father journal

FIVE YEARS OF AWAKENING TO FATHERHOOD

By David Steinberg

TIMES CHANGE PRESS
Albion, CA 95410

Copyright © 1977 by David Steinberg

Printed in the U.S.A.
Second Printing

Times Change Press
Albion, CA 95410

●

Library of Congress Cataloging in Publication Data
Steinberg, David, 1942-
   Fatherjournal: five years of awakening to fatherhood

1. Steinberg, David, 1942-
2. Fathers—Biography.
3. Father and child.
   I. Title.
HQ756.S783   301.42'7   77-5908
ISBN 0-87810-534-4 hardbound
ISBN 0-87810-034-2 paperback

●

Times Change Press material is copyrighted to prevent reprinting by profit-making publishers. When possible, we readily give permission for its use by people whose purpose is, like ours, to help further personal growth and radical social change.

●

Acknowledgements:
   The September 15, 1971, entry is excerpted from "Fatherhood: Notes at Six Months," which originally appeared in *The Future of the Family*, Louise Kapp Howe, editor, Simon and Schuster, 1972.
   Six poems ("Goodbye father-dream," "Lovely, loving bath with Dylan," "Voices drift up the stairs," "Dylan sleeps softly," "The books say it is a stage," and "Seven times") are taken from *Welcome, Brothers: poems of a changing man's consciousness*, by David Steinberg, Red Alder Books, 1976.
   "I heard my nose break this morning" originally appeared in *Community of Friends*, Fall, 1975.
   "The plainest menorah, and wrong" originally appeared in *The Jewish Exponent*, June 25, 1976.

To all the fathers who have been taught to turn away from their children, and the growing numbers of fathers who are turning back.

Why I want to write a book on fathering:

– *because being a father is difficult and exciting, a highly charged part of my life.*

– *because I know there are many men who want to be closely involved with their children but who are afraid of that intimacy; who feel incompetent, awkward, and out of place; who are isolated and confused and don't know how to begin.*

– *because I am blown away by the anguish of men who lose their children through divorce or separation.*

– *because I want to encourage myself and other men to admit the depth and strength of our feelings about children, and to explore those feelings rather than suppress them and be eaten away by an unnamed sense of lost possibility.*

– *because children feel the distance of cold fathers deeply and work out those feelings all their lives – on their men friends and husbands – looking for their lost fathers or avoiding the disappointment of rejection.*

– *because of all the men's liberation issues this is the strongest self-interest issue for men.*

– *because I believe that men can be brought into contact with each other around this issue, and that that contact will provide support for re-evaluating male roles.*

– *because I want to make a clear statement about how I feel about being a father.*

– *because I want to make myself visible as a person who wants to work with men who are struggling with these issues.*

I feel like David facing Goliath: so much to begin, so much to unravel. I know so little. I must learn as much as I can. Read, talk to people who have thought about fathering, share with other men. Yes, that feels right. The tears clear from my eyes, then return. I pray for strength and wisdom.

David, get up.

Get up, David.

'Cause the light is outside,

because the sun is shining orange.

It's time to get up

because it's morning.

        Dylan, August 30, 1973

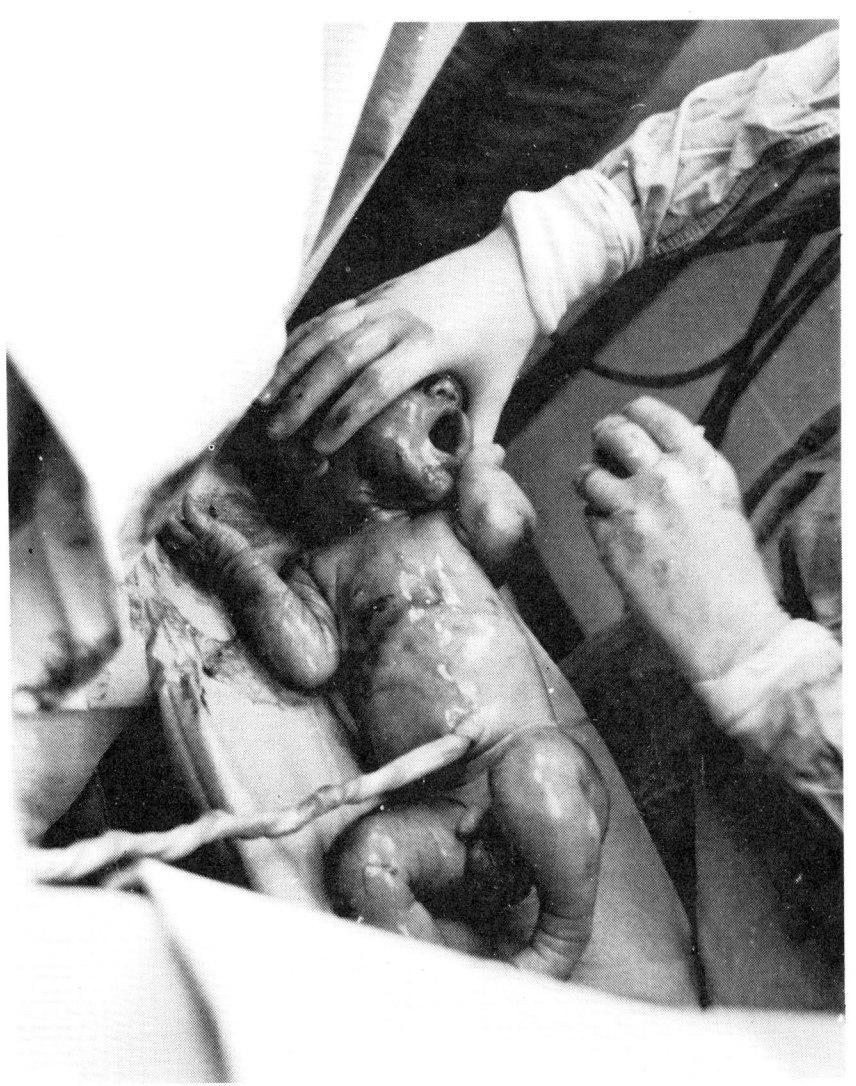

April 1, 1971 (San Francisco)

Woke up — 3:00 a.m. Started timing contractions.

3:02 — 3 min. 3:16 — 40 sec. 3:20 — 10 sec. 3:26 — 35 sec. 3:30 — 10 sec. 3:34 — 25 sec. 3:36 — 30 sec. 3:38 — 35 sec. 3:44 — 35 sec. 3:48 — 40 sec. 3:55 — 60 sec. 4:02 — 20 sec. 4:05 — 20 sec. 4:10 — 30 sec. 4:12 — 25 sec. 4:14 — 30 sec. 4:20 — 30 sec. 4:25 — 40 sec. 4:30 — 45 sec. 4:36 — 40 sec. 4:40 — 30 sec. 4:45 — 45 sec. 4:48 — 45 sec.

Decided to go to hospital — 4:00.
Left home — 4:40.
Arrived at hospital — 5:00.
Susan's prep began — 5:25.
Prep finished by 6:05.
Susan began pushing at 7:00.
Into delivery room — 7:22.
DYLAN JOSHUA — 7:32 a.m.
For unto us a child is born, unto us a son is given.

Portalwood Drug Store has Swedish milk cups.

Buy cotton, alcohol.

Bring back to hospital: pacifier, book, camera, dress for Susan, nightgown, undershirt, receiving blanket, regular blanket, diapers, pins.

April 3, 1971

Baby home. At last he's asleep, after two meals and lots of screaming. Rococo music on the radio relaxes me. The baby's not into sleeping very much. Sucking. He's really into sucking.

I'm feeling weary already, after just an hour of taking care of the baby. One minute I feel fine, the next exhausted. Why exhausted? I'm not doing that much, and I don't feel overly nervous or tense. Just excitement, I guess.

Curry the cat hasn't even noticed that Dylan is here yet.

April 18, 1971 (lullaby)

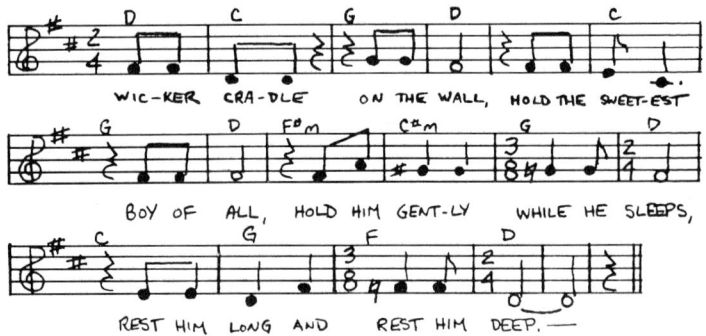

Wicker cradle on the wall,
Hold the sweetest babe of all,
Hold him gently while he sleeps,
Rest him long and rest him deep.

Happy mobile hanging high,
Watch the cradle from the sky.
Draw the good warm feelings in,
Keep your peace sign over him.

Pretty babe, asleep at last,
Dreaming dreams of colors past,
If you cry what will I do?
Let my heart song comfort you.

Quiet music for the boy,
Gentle sounds of quiet joy.
Pretty baby, wrapped in blue,
Pretty baby, I love you.

May 2, 1971

Tonight I cried for the first time since Dylan was born. All the walls, all the strengths, all the holding tight, came tumbling down and the tears came tumbling out.

I know so little of being a father. It is too much for me.

I was going to be the perfect father: loving, caring nurturing, soft. I was going to make up for all the men who leave the children to the women, who back away from intimacy with children, who are cold and distant. I was going to do it right.

Tonight I see how scared I am. There is so much to do for this little creature who screams and wriggles and needs and doesn't

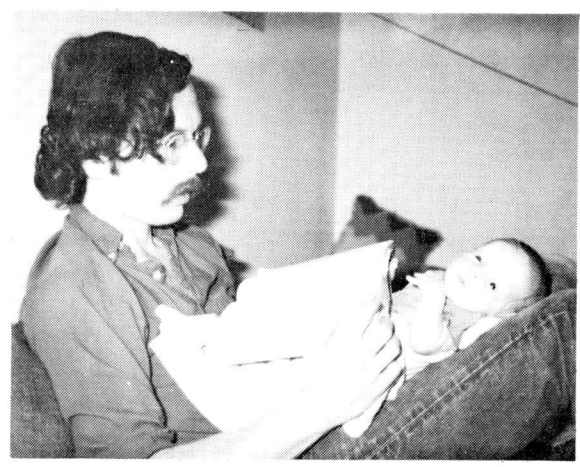

know what he needs and relies on me to figure it all out. I watch myself run away, leaving the baby to Susan and her woman's intuition and her breasts full of milk. Part of me wants to get as far away from him as I possibly can. Sitting in the armchair while Susan struggled to get him to sleep, I finally admitted how far I am from where I would like to be.

I tried to tell Susan what was going on with me. It was hard to talk. He's only been here a month, and already it's more than I can handle. I cried for a long, long time. It felt good to confess, to break down.

Afterwards I had the beginnings of a new vision: I need to accept my fear, my reluctance, my instinct to flee. I have to start from where I am instead of where the model new-age father would be. Susan encouraged me to let myself run away when I needed to. It helped to hear that from her, since she will be left to take care of Dylan whenever I do.

I am so small compared to what needs to be done.

August 10, 1971

> Shadows on the sand
> where the sea has come and gone
> leaving its memory in dark wedges.
> Mist overhead,
> white waves against the green sea,
> and a huge wet rat lying dead on its side.
>
> I am the city:
> > running
> >> pushing
> >
> > yelling
> >> screaming
> >
> > and under everything the ocean

    washing again and again
    onto the beach.

Opening the door,
there is so much sadness
just to find a little joy.

    Descending night sucks the air and the strength of this afternoon out of me. I run to the Family Farmacy, fleeing the vacuum. The dread and the panic.

    When I stop running I see the vacuum and it scares me. But stopping also makes room for me to grow in ways that are separate from the running, the constant motion, the compulsive activity. So many changes are going on in me right now. I am changing speeds, discovering a whole new sense of myself, a whole new way of being. Somehow it is all related to having a new-born baby. It scares me to death. How shall I live without being who I have been?

    I feel better just writing this. I find company in the ink that flows onto the page, shaped into words. There is a quiet, sane, strong, warm feeling in this hip cafe tonight. Thank God.

    Peter Spellman sings soft music. Welcome. "You got to go with it/ you got to flow with it/ turn your life over to the rhythm of the magic band." Good music talking, teaching. A mantra for these times. "Your presence gave me strength when I was tired/ your caring brought me out from being insane/ now what I want is to be with you again."

    Up and down and up again. I'm getting seasick. It is a time of change. Turbulence of a new front moving in. Rumble of dry air passing...

    Man-woman, your ocean heartbeat
    arranges the sand of my shore.

August 21, 1971

I have spent most of my time running, avoiding, shutting things out. This is the energy I have used to "accomplish things." It is the need to keep busy: if I stop who knows what will come popping out. It is the need to keep myself under control.

Now, as having a baby tears apart my ability to control my life, I begin to explore the possibility of letting go. I learn a little about following instead of leading, about slowing down, about listening, about responding to what's going on around me and inside me.

I'm excited by this new exploring, but I'm also reluctant to let go of the old sense of accomplishment that requires more speed, more control. I'm afraid that if I let go of that driving energy I will become mediocre, common, uninteresting, unlovable. I'm afraid that if I don't push myself I'll never do anything.

It's a question of who I want to be. I'm trying too hard—with Dylan, with Susan, with writing, with everything. It's making me miserable. Now I try not to try. Last week I began being better to myself. This week I'm better yet. It helps to remember how much I like myself when I relax.

September 15, 1971 (notes at six months)

Dylan is napping: a chance to unwind and settle into writing. I still find it hard to write in tune with Dylan's schedule. Like now I've just started and he's woken up crying. I have to stop and take care of him.

When Susan was pregnant, I imagined that writing and taking care of the baby would fit together well. I figured that as long as I was home taking care of the baby I would do some writing as well. It seems incredible now that I could have so completely misunderstood what it would be like to have a baby.

I have resisted the shift from living on my schedule to living on Dylan's. I've tried to hold on to my old patterns, failed, and built up a lot of resentment in the process. After six months I think I'm finally letting go of my old life. The task is to build a new life that I like as well or better. One day, at the ocean, I cried while trying to say goodbye to a life that I loved and had worked hard to create.

Having a baby has brought an astounding amount of day-to-day work. A lot gets lost in the shuffle, like having time to sit and relax, time to talk about things that are hard to say, time to sort out feelings and become whole again. There are no more Sunday morning breakfasts in bed.

I wish now that I had prepared myself better for having a baby. I let myself get caught by surprise, and then felt resentful, as if I had been cheated out of something I couldn't quite define.

I'm not willing to be the second, somewhat foreign, parent. I tried that for a couple of days in a pique of frustration with Dylan. I felt distant and alienated from him almost immediately. It was horrible. Better to share responsibility for him, whatever the frustration.

Susan and I agree that we'll both work part-time and share taking care of Dylan. That way we'll both have outside lives and both be involved parents.

I still get an empty feeling when people ask me what I'm doing. Most of my energy in the last six months has focused on Dylan—on taking care of him and getting used to his being here. I carry enough man-work expectations in me that I feel uncomfortable using that to identify myself to people.

Having Dylan has made me feel confused, overwhelmed, uncertain—then bitter and resentful. The feeling of being up against something that I can't handle, that is too much for me. So many things need to be done, so many emotional places need to be put together, and my energy outside of Dylan is so very, very low. Life has become complicated. I feel the jaws of middle-aged American mediocrity open wide.

Often my anger and frustration come out at Susan. It seems ridiculous to rage at Dylan, and I'm too defensive to blame myself.

I'm an only child, and I never babysat as a teenager. I knew nothing about babies when Dylan was born. My confidence in myself as a father was very shaky. I could hold myself together as long as everything went smoothly, but when something unusual happened I panicked. I got very depressed at my lack of intuitive baby sense.

Once I admitted all that to myself, and to Susan, I could face my weaknesses and work on them. I began to see that there were times when I was really good with Dylan, when I really did have good intuitive sense about relating to a baby.

I wanted to jump right in, confident and competent, and be a father who thoroughly enjoyed taking care of his baby. I wanted to cut all the American father bullshit out of me in one slice. But overcoming basic cultural habits isn't that easy or dramatic. Now, after six months' work, I can see that the transition is happening after all. And that makes me feel that it's been worth all the trauma and tension.

As soon as I get oriented to one of Dylan's patterns, he

changes and a whole new pattern begins to evolve. It's like standing up in a roller coaster. I'm finding that the more I accept this constant change, the more I can enjoy the dynamics of it, the constant growing. Dylan is deepening my sense of change as a way of life.

I can't impose my rules on Dylan. All the persuasive skills I use to get other people to do things my way are totally irrelevant to him. I am forced to accept the validity of his rules, and then learn to integrate that with my real needs. The trick is to become less of a control freak without entirely sacrificing myself to Dylan.

I know I will make major mistakes with Dylan, that I'll cause him a great deal of real grief. I try to keep that in front of me, to accept it when it happens.

Susan wanted a have a baby at least a year before I did. Being a father was a frightening thought to me. I kept waiting to be more together, to have my life somehow be more resolved. Susan said that I could wait forever if I wanted things to be perfect, that the only way to feel good about being a father was to have a baby and work through the hassles. I was persuaded. We decided to have a baby. Susan became pregnant immediately.

I've often thought that we should have waited a little longer, maybe another year. Maybe then the adjustment wouldn't have been so traumatic. On the other hand it may be that adjusting to a baby is traumatic by nature and that it would have been just as hard a year later.

While Susan was pregnant my relationship with her, and with myself, went through a beautiful time of growing and deepening. It was a very exciting time. I think now that I was getting ready for Dylan, unconsciously preparing for the upheaval that my conscious mind refused to acknowledge.

It's easy to spend all my time sitting around the house. Doing things with Dylan often seems so complicated. On the other hand, the more we try with him the more seems possible. He sleeps well in strange places, and survives late night trips home on the bus. He bounces around the city in his back pack, goes on long car trips peacefully, and has enjoyed camping out, diapers and all, for a week at a time.

It's always a shock when I remember that Dylan is related to me in a more basic way than that I take care of him. To realize that he is of my body, grown from my seed. He is my son. Occasionally that realization hits me from behind. I still don't know what to make of it. I suffer from not having been pregnant.

Dylan has been sleeping for three hours while I've been writing. Susan has gone to her bus driving job. When he wakes up he's going to be hungry. I'd better go make a bottle.

Most of our friends don't have babies and don't relate to Dylan very warmly. I remember that before Dylan was born I was easily annoyed by the demands of friends' babies. I can see how couples with babies tend to socialize with each other almost exclusively. Still, I don't want to give up my relationships with friends who don't have kids. We'll have to work something out.

Being with Dylan gives me a chance to express my intuitive, feminine, yin self. It's easy for a man to always be in situations that call for aggressive, rational, manipulative perspectives and skills. With Dylan I move out of that more completely than I ever have before. The obvious importance of these new skills in relating to Dylan helps me respect and value them as they develop.

All in all, I now enjoy most of the time I spend with Dylan—taking care of him, playing with him, watching him change and grow. He is one of the most important parts of my life. There are other important parts—my relationship with Susan, my work, being with other people. I don't want to give them up for Dylan, or him for them. I look for the balance, remembering that there is as much total space in my life as I have energy to keep clear.

October 18, 1971

At the Family Farmacy with Dylan, a spontaneous excursion into the land of Why Not. Why not just take him and get out of the house? I put him in the back pack, with all the gear. We hitchhiked easily to Market Street with a delightful man who was as fascinated with Dylan as Dylan was with him. Then we took a bus, meeting a lovely, crazy woman who also flashed on Dylan. Now Dylan rests on the floor, playing happily with his pink teething ring. All smooth so far.

When we got here I was reluctant to actually go in. I've never seen any other babies at this place. What would people think? What if he decided to start screaming when I took my first sip of coffee? Then I decided to take the plunge. I told myself I could always leave if he got outrageous.

As it is, Dylan is being wonderful and I'm enjoying the feeling of being out with him. A new freedom taken. I sense that it really is possible to make space for what I need. It means flowing with what's happening, being prepared to change plans at any moment. Like yesterday when we packed up to go to the beach only to have Dylan decide to take a nap when we got to the ocean. We sat and talked in the car, watching the waves until he woke up. It was a good warm time with Susan, but one that we could easily have lost to the frustration of not being able to follow the plans we had set for ourselves. Again, the issue is letting go of control over my life. How to let go of the need to control the trivia and still hang on to what's really important to me?

October 20, 1971

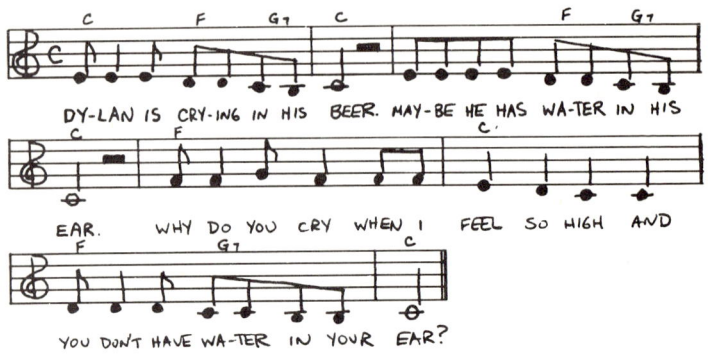

Dylan is crying in his beer.
Maybe he has water in his ear.
Why do you cry when I feel so high
And you don't have water in your ear?

Dylan is crazy as a loon,
Funny as an old baboon.
If we can get him into tune
Maybe someday he'll play bassoon.

I don't know how to sing this song.
Seems like it's going much too long.
Don't make it into right or wrong,
I just don't know how to sing this song.

Time for singing, sing a new song,
Maybe you will sing along with me.
We'll have to see.
Pretty baby, eyes so wide,
What is going on inside your head?
Dylan peppers, who are you
With your coat so blue?
Since the very first day you came
Things have never been the same.
Now you're screaming, something is wrong,
Maybe you don't like my song to you.
What can I do?

Bouncing baby, bouncing up high,
Maybe you will reach the sky someday.

It's hard to say.
Are you sleepy? Hanging your head,
Maybe you would like to go to bed.
When you're crying, when you're blue,
You know it hurts me too.
If I knew just what I should do,
I would surely do it for you.
Now you're quiet, going to sleep,
Maybe I won't hear a peep from you
Til half past two.

October 26, 1971

Yesterday was a beautiful free day, a gift from Walt and Pam who called to say they would like to take Dylan for a day. Just like that, a day off. A chance to be alone together. We dropped Dylan off and took the ferry to Sausalito, wandering around, feeling lazy and free, following our noses to nowhere in particular. Corned beef sandwiches, a bookstore's wonderment, peach milk shakes, drinks on the outdoor patio of the No Name Bar, sitting on the sea wall watching the bay. When the boat got back to the dock in San Francisco there was a bluegrass band to welcome us, a reminder that there is real beauty left in the city of cable cars, Victorian houses, and once-flower children.

At the bookstore I found this quote from Gibran: "When you are covered with darkness, look at it as dawn being born."

Amen.

November 3, 1971 (New York)

A long-distance excursion, just me and Dylan. We are in New York to visit my parents for a week, while Susan gets a week to be free and alone.

I prepared myself carefully for the five-hour plane ride and was ready to devote all of my energy and attention to doing whatever Dylan needed to have done. Several trips to the "lavatory-vacant," juggling him on the closed toilet seat while changing diapers in the jiggly little space. Walking him up and down the skinny aisle. Watching him play peek-a-boo with the people in the seats behind us. It became a challenge and I felt triumphant. Dylan was happy, slept part of the way stretched out at my feet, was not overly demanding.

The stewardesses didn't know what to make of us. They tended to assume that I needed a lot of their feminine help. I was determined to put the torch to that bullshit, and I pulled it off. Good for me.

Got some nice hits from an older couple who seemed to appreciate that I was by myself taking an infant cross-country. They weren't condescending like the stewardesses, just friendly and appreciative. They probably assumed that I was a single father.

On this trip I'm enjoying the feeling of being fully responsible for Dylan. He is a focus for my energy, a fixed point around which I can orient myself. Having nothing else that I need to do I am free to just be with Dylan. It feels good, and I sense that Dylan likes it too.

November 4, 1971 (New York)

> Goodbye father-dream,
> it's time for you to go.
>> Sad.
> I have missed you as I waited
> sometimes angry, sometimes hopeful,
> passionate and patient.
>> Now I see that you're not coming,

indisposed as it were,
and there are other things to do:
>   my living life calls.
I'll go now and leave this map
so you can find me
if you should happen to pass this way.

I came to you
open and eager
not knowing that by holding out my hand
I could bring you such pain,
twisting the knife you hold so tightly
between your ribs.
You would have been better off without me,
your knives would have melted sooner.
How tired I am of having my existence
make you afraid.
I will take what you offer
and build my expectations elsewhere.
I, too, must survive.

God bless Dylan for staying asleep while I wrote. It helps to get that feeling out in words. Something about being here alone with Dylan has tuned me in to some buried feelings about my father. It is good to see all that a little more clearly. A step beyond longing for a closeness that was missing in the past. A step toward working out what level of intimacy is possible in the present. It helps to accept that there are real limits. I feel my anger dissolving. Right now I feel peaceful. Sad and peaceful.

Dylan wakes in quiet good humor. Time to go out into the sunshine and explore New York.

Clear, cold crispy-crunchy day in the big city. Dylan is rested and joyful as we go off together into the glorious day.

Walking along 86th Street we draw smiles and more than a few stares from passing people. Are we that unusual? I check Dylan to be sure he's warm enough (he has only a light jacket on). I find that he's in great shape, warm as toast. He looks over my shoulder from his lime-green pack, taking in the sights and sounds and feels of the city. He stares up at the tall buildings like any tourist (or is it the street lamp that's caught his eye?), then turns to watch passing people over his shoulder. Women who pass with babies look at Dylan. I smile to them, but there is no contact between them and me.

The buildings grow taller and squarer and then we're in Central Park, following a little path through trees and fallen leaves that mix green and yellow. The leaves are soft from the rain and still alive. It's not yet time for them to be brown and crunchy. Dylan is quietly absorbed, so still in fact that I check to make sure he's alive and well, which he completely is.

After a while Dylan gets hungry and we find a bench for his mid-morning meal. A clogged nipple is remedied by a friendly woman's hairpin. We talk babies while Dylan eats. She tells me she doesn't like overprotective mothers and overdressed babies. She does like crisp weather and walking in the light rain when "everyone stays indoors and you have New York to yourself." Her daughter, Erika, is nine months old. She demonstrates her collapsable baby-wheeler to me. Erika laughs on and off. Then it's time for them to go.

When Dylan has finished eating we head for the warmth of the Museum of Natural History. We wander inside the huge building with thousands of boisterous schoolchildren, teachers, parent aides, and museum guides. Dylan takes it all in—the noise, the dark halls, the displays, the people. We stop for a quick cafeteria lunch. Dylan babbles and laughs and plays with my purple pen. Then out again through another crowd of school kids to the crosstown bus.

On the bus Dylan talks and yells while I admire the long

auburn hair of the woman in front of us. The bus rushes us homeward. The woman gets off to catch the subway. When we get home, Dylan promptly goes to sleep. I read the last of Ray Mungo's book and then settle down comfortably on the couch to write this. What a wonderful afternoon! Now for a nap...

November 30, 1971

Once there was a little boy who fell into a hole.
Over, under, over, under, over he did roll.
And he rolled so far from his sweet bed,
He came to the bottom and he bumped his head.

There he met a genie, and the genie's name was Joe.
Joe the genie who knew everything there was to know.
And the genie, Joe, said, "Make a wish,
Do you want a broiler or a chafing dish?"

The little boy considered how this wishing should be done.
A million things to wish for and he only could have one.
After thinking near and thinking far
He said to Joe, "Please bring me an electrical guitar."

Joe the genie laughed and laughed and said, "I've just
     the thing,
A very special Gibson that will make the heavens ring."
Then he clapped his hands, and when he spoke,
Everything was covered with a puff of smoke.

Genie Joe was right, it was a magical guitar,
The sound of which could reach up to the very furthest star.
And the people came from miles around
To dance and to sing to the happy sound.

The little boy he played and played upon the village square,
And soon there were a hundred million billion people there.
With a microphone and special lights
He played for seven days and he played for seven nights.

After seven days the little boy could play no more.
His voice was cracked and broken and his fingers they were
     sore.
So he packed his case and went away.
"Powerfully moving!" the reviewers all did say.

January, 1972: I take a job, full-time, as editor of a column on alternative lifestyles for newspapers. The job is nine-to-five, and involves a 40-minute commute from San Francisco to Palo Alto. Susan, who has been driving a bus part-time for a school for emotionally distrubed children, quits that job to take care of Dylan so I can do the editorial *work. We agree to work through the difficulties of my working full-time so I can do this job, which looks like just the kind of work I want to do. As it turns out, the job is not all that exciting, and after six months the project folds.*

January 10, 1972

Today is the first foggy morning in ages. I welcome it with a feeling of open, deep, quiet sadness. The Oberlin College Choir sings softly, and Dylan is asleep. It is exceptionally still. The craziness is gone. In its place is this thick sadness. I like it much better than the frenzy. It feels more real somehow. I take this chance to unwind, to breathe deeply. Chores can be done later.

I realize how much I have been living in the future, waiting for something to begin instead of being alive now. It's one of the things I do when I get overwhelmed. I feel myself reaching, trying, pushing things to happen most of the time. The rhythm of letting, receiving, accepting, flowing gets shut out. It's like the puzzle where you stick your fingers in both ends and the harder you try to pull them out, the tighter the trap gets.

It's been a long time since I've done things richly, with delicacy and art. Adjusting to Dylan has hit me like a tidal wave, and I've been struggling just to keep my head above water. I certainly haven't had time to be relaxed and open, even though I know that being closed and tense just makes the rest of my life more difficult.

Saturday I began to feel that things were basically all right again, that my life makes sense even though so many parts of it are pulling against each other. Being in a valley doesn't mean that I've taken the wrong road, just that all roads have valleys.

Dylan sleeps long when my mind is peaceful like this. Is it just coincidence? Maybe it's that when I use time well there's enough of it after all.

February 20, 1972

    This morning I woke up feeling comfortable, warm, and solid. Then Dylan started to fuss and I turned irritable right away. I wake up to a demand every morning. I'm behind before I even get out of bed. A horrible way to start the day.
    Maybe on weekends, when I don't have to go to work, I should spend some time by myself before getting up officially. Use my two free mornings to pull myself together instead of for sleeping. Take a little time to just sit and compose myself, let the dust settle, breathe slower, still the eddies that have been spinning in my brain.

(lullaby)

If you're tired go to sleep and close your eyes,
When you wake I'll be right here beside you.
Put your head on my arm,
Let my body keep you warm,
In your dreams there'll be sunny skies,
Go to sleep and close your eyes.

March 12, 1972

Dylan is an incredibly wonderful child! After sleeping for an hour he's been playing contentedly by himself for 30 minutes now. He's friendly, fun to watch, fun to play with. Yesterday I was alone with him all day and I loved it. Things are definitely getting better.

Seven adjectives for Dylan at 11 months: playful, inquisitive, strong inside, persistent, funny, happy, responsive.

March 20, 1972

Gordon Lightfoot sings his gentle, lonely songs. I don't have time to write many songs these days. I miss the quiet morning hour I had when Dylan was still taking morning naps.

Today Dylan is sick and weird. High fever, fussy, lethargic. He's still adorable though when he gets a little energy together. Such an amazing fellow.

I get so parentally worried when Dylan gets sick. What can we do? What if he gets worse? Susan and I pore over the books trying to figure out what's going on with him. It's terrible to think of something being wrong with him. My God... What if... Maybe he's...

April 1, 1972

It is a quiet, grey Saturday. Dylan's first birthday. Dylan is being wonderful and adorable. All dressed in his red shirt and yellow overalls he stands here playing with the spiral binding of my notebook and says "Dadadada." From time to time he bobs up and down to Judy Collins' singing and wants my attention, which is only fair...

One minute later and all that peace and good feeling is completely destroyed. How can everything change so quickly? Dylan turns obnoxious. My parents call to say how sick they are, while Dylan cries more. I get off the phone but he won't stop crying, and suddenly I'm going crazy out of my mind again. Finally I take him out for a walk, having exhausted every other thought about what to do, and now he's fine again. But I'm all clenched up and a little nauseous. I want to yell, "Unfair! Unfair!"

April 8, 1972

Seven adjectives for Dylan at one year: cheerful, curious, active, independent, imitative, reckless, pleased with himself.

April 21, 1972

Start at the beginning: I feel tense, frustrated, angry, irritable. Dylan is fussing, as he's been doing all afternoon. I wish he would just disappear for a while. He won't.

Yesterday was my day off. I got to sit around and take care of Dylan all afternoon while Susan ran errands. Today I get to rush home from work and sit with Dylan while Susan goes to Kaiser to see a doctor about her chest pains. And I can look ahead to a glorious weekend of sitting around this dumb house feeling pent up, doing nothing, while Dylan screams continuously and drives me nuts.

Then in the evening when Dylan goes to sleep I get to hear about how empty Susan's life is. If I read, Susan feels neglected. I never have any time just to be alone in peace. How can I get myself together when I never have any free space? Sorry, no room for growing any more, you're got a baby now. Well, fuck that!

Today I had a fantasy of clipping Dylan under the chin, a pure energy uppercut with my knee. I could see his head snap back and his body topple over and his head hit the floor. The fantasy felt good when it happened. Now retelling it makes me want to cry. Is this what having a child is all about? Is this what working full-time is all about? What do other people do when they have feelings like these?

It seems that whenever I'm really down like this, Susan's response is to get angry. Sorry, David, stop whining, be strong. This morning I yelled at Dylan when he got on my nerves, and then I didn't feel like picking him up to comfort him. Susan thought I must be an ogre to be so inconsiderate of this dear sweet baby. She, on the other hand, keeps all her resentments about Dylan bottled up until she can throw them all off on me.

I want time alone. What keeps me from arranging that? I feel sorry for Susan who's all alone all day taking care of sick Dylan and being bored. I should be willing to help her deal with all that but it's hard to sympathize with her when she just gets mad at me whenever I'm upset.

> *May, 1972: After months of talk and plans, we move from San Francisco to Boulder Creek, a small town in the Santa Cruz Mountains. We buy a small house outside of town and a little open land. It is the first time I have ever lived outside of a city, except for college. I continue working in Palo Alto, commuting an hour each way.*

June 18, 1972

Susan is off camping for a few days. It has been a good, fun, finally tiring day—just me and Dylan and the country. Doing the laundry in town, taking a long bike ride far up into the hills. Dylan has been wonderful. I've enjoyed being in charge of him again.

Yesterday a song came for the first time in months. I had thought the songwriting was gone forever.

June 30, 1972

Alone in the country. Susan and Dylan have gone off to Pennsylvania for a week to visit her parents. I hesitate to write. I'm feeling so weird.

I want to let go but I'm afraid. Afraid I'll start to cry and cry forever. I carry around a dammed reservoir of fear and I don't want it to wash me away. Instead I stay busy—do this, do that. What will happen if I stop?

I feel sticky and dried out. A shower would be beautiful. I'll go do that.

In the shower waves of crying came. I realized that my fear has to do with sex. Before Dylan was born I was becoming open to my body in a new way, getting past all the roles and the bullshit that gets everything so turned around. Then Dylan came and all that new good feeling disappeared. How infuriating and frustrating that has been—moving with Susan into a good, open sexual place only to have Dylan's birth interrupt all that with a new level of difficulty. There are no more quiet afternoons together. Both of us feel tense and overwhelmed most of the time, and tired at night. I have resented Dylan for that more than anything else. And I am afraid to do all the work to open those heavy doors again.

> *July, 1972: My job in Palo Alto ends. I am free to spend more time at home, more time with Dylan. I start collecting unemployment insurance.*

> *September, 1972: Susan begins to do some substitute teaching and to play organ at two churches nearby.*

October 15, 1972

I woke up this morning to find that Susan had already gone down to the Mountain Store and brought back the Sunday paper. What a nice surprise! We had eggs and sausages for breakfast. I felt very country—eating, reading the paper, listening to the rain.

Dylan and I played together with his blocks for a long time this morning. We built twisted piles when he was in charge, and towering, symmetrical facades when it was my turn to pile the blocks. Eventually each tower would fall and we'd both yell "Crash!" and laugh and clear space to start again.

Then we got into hammering pegs. First me, then Dylan, whichever he preferred. He swings the hammer super hard, makes all the noise he can, gets more and more excited with each stroke. Often he ends up whacking his head or his eye on the backstroke. That stops him for a minute, but then he's at it again, just as careless and unrestrained as before. It's great to be with him that way. I realize how seldom I take time to play with him around *his* games, *his* interests.

October 16, 1972

At an army surplus store I found an old dial and bought it for Dylan. You turn the axle and the numbers go around inside a window. 0, 10, 20... Dylan was delighted when I gave it to him. I thought he would be. He kept saying, "Look! Look!" I felt wonderful.

October 18, 1972

A good day alone with Dylan. It was sunny most of the time, and quite warm. We walked a lot. Down to the bridge to look at the swollen, muddy creek. Then into the woods where the ground was all covered with wet pine needles. Soft, damp, quiet, orange-brown. The big fir tree that fell has blocked the old path. We scouted a new one. Dylan enjoyed it, alive and relaxed, and so did I.

Dylan is really getting comfortable in the woods now. He roamed free over the pine needles, pushing low branches out of his way without hesitation. Quite a change from when he wouldn't

even let me go into the woods with him in the back pack.

Later, Susan and I decided to go out, to take an evening away from home, together and alone. A chance to relax and talk about the things we only talk about when we are out. We talked about Dylan and about not taking every little thing he does so very seriously. About loosening the reins of control, going with his flow, having a good time, not being so plagued by the ghosts of parental responsibility. I got clearer on the whole power trip I've been in with Dylan. It was good to talk.

December, 1972: I begin working again, part-time, in a job whose hours I can shape. The job is to organize and lead group workshops about work and money for the New Vocations Project of the American Friends Service Committee in San Francisco. Most of the time I work at home. Susan and I are back on the game plan: each working part-time, each taking care of Dylan part-time.

December 13, 1972

Tonight just loving Dylan, that's all. Rolling together, taking the time to really *see* him. Me beaming, filling the room with warmth and goodness. And Dylan soaking it up, rich and soft, all the spastic craziness gone, leaving him peaceful, a calm blue water facing an open sky.

All evening I kept crying. Rich, warm, overflowing feelings running out through my eyes. I just let the feeling keep moving me along, like a stick floating on a river. Just being with Dylan, knowing what's right without question or reason.

So much is possible with Dylan. So much that I can do, that I can be. Tonight I am open, alive, almost trembling with the richness that comes to me from Dylan. Joan Baez sings with the delicacy of crystal. I feel the warmth of the orange and black fire, the silence and peace of the country night. Sad-eyed lady of the lowlands. Liquid rising in my chest, filling me.

If I can be so alive and dizzy with the wonder of it now, why do I ever step away into the deathly, crazy, nonsense, non-sensing existence?

February 22, 1973

Dylan and I are so close in temperament. It amazes me

sometimes. We seem to resonate, to pick up each other's vibrations, all the time. We even get hungry at the same time, and I always know what he wants to eat. Unfortunately we also get tired and grouchy at the same time.

Today Dylan was as gentle as I felt, singing Genie Joe to his doll, playing with the blackboard we made him for Christmas. Very peaceful.

I should be writing a brochure for the free schools workshop, but I want to savor this good feeling. It is a nice reunion.

> *About play groups:* Since Dylan was about a year old he's been in one or another play group. Two or three or four kids play together, and each family is responsible *for the group one day a week. The kids get to know each other really well, and become intimate with several different adults. The parents get free time and the perspective of knowing other children. And it doesn't cost a cent.*

May 9, 1973

Play group day. I sit in the sun while the three boys amuse themselves in the sandbox. I might as well take the time to sit while I can get it. It can all change at any moment.

Like this morning when I was feeling good until I came across a pile of loose shit on the deck, then more on Leifin's shoes, and more yet in his pants. He had diarrhea, and no diapers on! What a mess. I was furious, at Beth for sending Leifin over without diapers and not telling me, and also at whichever kid had the bad luck to cross my path.

I need to get back in touch with Dylan. He's been whiny and demanding, and I snap at him all the time. I don't like striking out at him like that. It gets to where he's always a little afraid of me. But it's such an instantaneous reflex that I don't know quite how to control it.

Sometimes I just want to crawl into a shell and hibernate. Where to find the energy to turn around and work it all out?

After all, I tell myself, everything is in good shape. I have more free time than before, summer is beautiful, all goes well with my writing. It is a time of peace; I should enjoy it. But even the peaceful times are different than they were before Dylan was born. Peace with Dylan is an active and happy peace. I miss the peace of relaxed silence, of being free of demands, of unselfconsciously lazy days.

How can I create time like that? Maybe tomorrow I'll put everything aside and let myself just putter around Santa Cruz. Or take a vacation with Susan on Friday. Maybe an adventure. That would be fun. I want to kiss this melancholy, overwhelmed sadness goodbye.

The boys have wandered off. Guess I'll tag along.

August 27, 1973

Tonight while I was getting Dylan ready for bed he said, "I love you, David, when you do that."

I was confused. "When I do what?"

"When you put on my jamies."

Golly gee.

August 30, 1973

This morning, still half asleep, I heard this from Dylan:

"David, get up. Get up, David. 'Cause the light is outside. Because the sun is shining orange. It's time to get up because it's morning."

And then he went on: "Get up, David. I want you to get up. Get up. Please get up. I'll help you get up. You're so heavy! You're so heavy! Get up, David. Let me take off your blanket. Now get up. Get up by yourself."

I got up, smiling.

September 23, 1973

A break in the weather, so I have come to the park with Dylan. A chance for him to play playground games, and for me to sit and write and be around other people. Lots of young mothers, young children, and me.

It's strange being a man in this woman's place. There is an easy-going exchange among the women here, yet I am outside of it. The closeness among the women just doesn't include me.

I guess I'm jealous. These mothers share stories and support. Yet if I start a conversation with one of them there is an edge. Who is this man? What does he want? Why is he here?

Maybe it's all in my head, just me being uncomfortable about integrating this lunch counter. Whatever it is, it leaves me feeling strange and alone. I don't want to make people uncomfortable, yet spending so much time with Dylan keeps putting me in these all-female-but-for-me situations.

Perhaps Dylan wonders why I sit here on the hill, separate, rather than jumping into the social flow as he does.

January 7, 1974

Susan is off for a week alone, a week of not having to deal with Dylan and me. As soon as she leaves we are hit by a short wet snowstorm—just a couple of inches, but more snow than this valley

has seen in 70 years, and it sends trees crashing everywhere, shutting off electricity, telephones, water, and the highway. Tonight Dylan and I will sleep home for the first time in four nights.

When it started snowing we went out to play in the white. Dylan had never seen snow before and he was enchanted. We walked out to the highway and hitched into town, sat at Dean's, drank hot chocolate and took in all the excitement.

Then we found that the road had closed and we had no way to get home. We went home with some people from Camp Joy and spent the night there. Trees were down everywhere, the streets were slippery, and it was starting to get dark. Dylan got scared and wet and cold and generally freaked out. I was carrying him, trying to keep his feet warm, comfort him, walk, wonder where we would sleep, and watch for falling trees—all at the same time. I had no idea what would happen next.

Gradually we got settled around the wood stove, got dry socks for Dylan. I tried to stay cool and show Dylan that it would all be ok. Finally he calmed down and stopped crying for the first time in what seemed like hours. He stayed huddled up against me for support.

Trees were going down every few minutes. You'd hear a crack that sounded like it was inches away and then wait to see if the roof fell in. I was just trying to cope, to keep Dylan secure and warm, and figure out how to get him fed and to sleep. We cooked tortillas for 15 people, two at a time, and got some sleeping bags. I was a mother protecting her children from danger.

Now we have been home for two hours, and order is coming back. The living room is warm and cozy in the yellow kerosene light, Dylan is comfortably asleep in his own sweet bed, and everything is quiet except for the sound of falling rain. I got a fire started, read a book to Dylan by firelight, changed him into warm sleeping clothes, let him fall asleep next to me on the floor, with his head on my chest, his hands tucked under my outstretched arm, foot nestled into my curled fingers. I lay still and let my thoughts wander, enjoying Dylan's weight and warmth, the company of his body next to mine.

After a while I got up to move him to bed. He woke up.
"What are you going to do?"
"I'm just putting you in your bed."
"Oh."
"Would you like that?"

He nodded. I watched him snuggle into the cold sheets, arranged the blankets while I juggled a flashlight, and gave him a final kiss, enjoying his trust that power or no power, heat or no heat, everything was fine. His trust in me to be able to take care of him.

Then riding that rush of energy, I straightened out the kitchen, swept the floor, put away Dylan's toys and clothes, brought firewood in for the morning, set pans out to gather rain water, made the bed, cleaned up my desk, fixed myself half a grapefruit. Now the fire warms the room and I sit here happy, independent, proud of myself—writing just for the hell of it before going to bed.

January 26, 1974

    I heard my nose break this morning
        door flung open hard
        in sudden explosion at Dylan's antics.
    Then running out, slamming doors,
        away, away,
    dissolve into watery bed
          I wish, I wish.

    Little voice
    from far away:
        "David, don't leave me..."

    I call softly, to reassure,
    but no need, he only wants to play.
    At the doorway he is all smiles.
        "Let's hide!"
    Then hearing my pain he comes up to me softly,
        watching with wide eyes.
    I hold him, almost desperately—
        the simple clarity of his vagabond
        love and concern.

January 27, 1974

      At the bottom of my barrel.
      Dylan shares an old man's bread
      feeds ducks and gulls
          simple straightforward pleasure
          in front of my nose
      yet a universe removed.

January 29, 1974

This is a hard time for Susan and me. We are adjusting who we are as a couple, holding on to each other less tightly, kicking out openings for more space. I am the initiator, Susan willing but not enthusiastic. We fight and hurt each other and lose the ability to see what's happening.

Last night, in the middle of tears and confusion and frustration, sitting on the floor by the fireplace, Susan said she wanted to live apart for a while. She had made up her mind that she needed space alone to be able to see which way was up. She said she couldn't handle being together right now. She said she wanted to take Dylan. Could she take Dylan? She didn't want to talk about it, she just wanted to know if she could take Dylan.

I was terrified. I couldn't speak. How had it come to this. Certainly there must be a way to fix things. Leave? Take Dylan?

"No, you can't take Dylan," I said.

"I need him," Susan cried.

"I need him too," I whispered.

Tug of war. We each pull on an arm. Dylan rips down the middle. Anything but that. Anything but losing Dylan. How have we come to this?

I push for more talk, to find some other way to resolve. My mind is gone. I have never been so afraid. I am going on pure reflex and some kind of desperate hope. Susan relents. We talk. She doesn't want to leave. She too is desperate. I see that clearer than before. We will work harder together. My frozen terror melts to tears. I'm still shaking when we go to bed.

February 15, 1974 (notes at three years)

Differences in me as a father now, compared to when Dylan was six months old: I have more confidence in my intuition about

Dylan; I am less threatened by the thought of him taking over my life; I am clearer about the positive effects of Dylan on me; I relate to Dylan in more consistent, stable ways.

I think I finally feel, way down in my gut, that I am a good father. I still do all sorts of things badly. But all in all, when I look at how I am with Dylan, I get a warm, glowing feeling that says this is something I do well.

Sometimes when I'm doing something with Dylan, or just watching him play, I get an overwhelming rush of love for him— pure appreciation of who he is—this incredibly open, honest, alive, present world-explorer who gets such intense joy out of so many little things in his life. I literally get choked up in my throat. Sometimes I cry at the beauty of being so much in love with him, and at the realization that these moments disappear as suddenly as they come, sinking under all the petty resentments and fears and busy-ness of my life.

I feel so vulnerable when I open the door to my deepest love for Dylan, when I let myself see how important he is to me. What if I lose him? What if Susan and I separate someday? Dylan is taking me into a more committed relationship than I have ever allowed before, even with Susan.

I encourage Dylan to be influenced by other people, both children and adults. He spends two or three days a week at play group, in environments shaped by parents who are quite different from me and Susan. I am excited when he comes home with something that he has obviously gotten from someone else, even if it's something that I don't particularly like. It's a reminder that I don't control who he is or what he experiences.

I don't get to talk about my feelings as a father with other men very much. Even the fathers I feel closest to seem far away in terms of how they relate to their kids. They are good fathers, emotionally involved with their children, but none are sharing primary day-to-day responsibility for their children as I do.

I have heard other men talk about the joys of fatherhood, about appreciating their children, but not about the doubts and the fears and the uncertainties. It's as if everyone wants to project a positive, confident image. Surely it's not just me that gets depressed at the bad-tasting patterns. Maybe other men don't feel these things as strongly as I do. Maybe their kids are less central to their lives. Maybe I should pull back from being so intimately tied to Dylan.

I still defer to Susan when it comes to dealing with Dylan. She responds more quickly and sympathetically than I do, and he has learned to turn to her first. I am timid to change that pattern. If Susan's response is different from mine, I usually figure she knows better than me. This is changing slowly over time. More and more these days I respond to Dylan without waiting to see what Susan will do. And I'm freer to object if she's doing something that seems really wrong to me.

When Dylan and I are alone, everything changes. Then the basic rules become the ones he and I set up, rules that let us find our mutual stride. These are the times when I feel best about who I am with Dylan, about who he is with me.

One part of this is that when Dylan and I are alone there's no question of letting responsibility for him slide over to Susan. I end up more involved with him, accept the responsibility, enjoy the contact. As a result I feel good about myself.

April 9, 1974

Peaceful play group today. The kids play imitative games, get muddy and wet, test each other and their physical limits. Not much is needed from me.

I like it when everything runs smoothly. Leifin and Trelawny make their bodies into bridges between the couch and the chest. Boogie and Dylan duck under them. Then they switch parts and repeat the dance.

May 12, 1974

> My son, the acrobat
> hangs and climbs and turns
> inventing tricks and tasks
> on life's playground
> to find out who he is.

Dylan takes a drink of water from the water fountain, chases two ducks into the water, laughs at their splashing and at his power. He patrols the edge of the duck pond vigorously. As I write, I half listen for the splash of him falling in, but his steps are sure and balanced.

June 2, 1974

Dylan and Boogie slide and climb together, energy released after two solid days of being indoors. The noon sun warms me, encourages me to come out, unfold and relax.

Dylan and Boogie want to go wade in the river. We go down to the river beach. I take off Dylan's pants. Once again he's the kid who's naked. I try to get Boogie to take his pants off too, but he resists my most gentle persuasion.

They go off. After a while Dylan comes over to say that all the other kids have their pants on. I ask if he wants his pants on. He says no. He asks if we brought short pants for him. We didn't, but I can roll up his long ones if he wants. I tell him I think it's nice to not have pants on. (Of course I have mine on.) "That's why I don't want any," he agrees. He pauses, standing close to me, working on the contradiction without resolving it. Slowly he goes off.

Soon he comes back again, definitely not all right. I ask if he wants his pants on. He does, and rolled down. He even asks to have his shirt on. Then he hangs close to me, still feeling very separate from the other kids. Meanwhile Boogie wades waist deep in the river, plays with a beach ball, runs around with the other kids.

Dylan wants to go home for something to drink. Boogie wants to stay. I want to stay too. We stay, despite Dylan's repeated complaints.

June 8, 1974 (Berkeley)

I'm at the Copper Penny—nice, plastic coffee house. I feel more comfortable here than in the supposedly intimate places. I like the open space, even the muzak.

At the crafts fair this afternoon I bought myself a batiked t-shirt. They had them for kids too, but I didn't think to buy one for Dylan. Something too cliché about a father coming home from a trip with a little present for his son. Now I wish I had bought one.

I missed Dylan a lot this afternoon. He was sad when I told him I wanted to take this trip alone instead of with him as I had promised. I needed the time by myself, and I'm glad I took the space I needed. But I'm sorry to have raised Dylan's expectations only to disappoint him.

As I was wandering around the fair I noticed a lost boy, maybe four years old. He was getting more upset by the minute as he looked and called for his mother. I went over to him (as I never do in these situations), gave him a big hug, and asked what was wrong. He stopped crying immediately, much to my surprise and relief. We walked around together, trying to find his mom. He was calm but as we came to the end of the circuit I got nervous about what to do next. I decided that we could sit and listen to the people playing music and just wait for her to appear.

Just then his mother came up, as if nothing unusual was going on. She made some remark to the boy about how silly he was to have wandered off and gotten worried, thanked me without much feeling, and took him off. I was amazed at how unaware she was of what was going on with her son. As they walked off into the crowd, he looked back at me one more time, and we exchanged a quiet look to say goodbye.

I will definitely get a shirt like mine for Dylan tomorrow.

I feel completely vulnerable to little children these days. It used to be just Dylan, but now I notice that I warm to other kids as well, especially to their sadness and disappointments.

I want to spend more time surrendered to Dylan, doing *his* things or things I know he would enjoy. Usually when we're together we do my things. That's ok, but it's different. It says that he's supposed to fit into my life if he wants us to be together. It says that being together is more important to him than it is to me. We could take a weekend trip together, come up here and go to Tilden Park or to the San Francisco Zoo or to the Lawrence Hall of Science. Or go to the Santa Cruz boardwalk for ice cream and rides, or to a kids' movie...

Oh Dylan, why am I only now beginning to let myself enjoy just being with you? Cheap resentment of your infringing on "my space?" I love you so much. I feel so unworthy of your total trust, and depressed to see your trust begin to fade because I'm not always there for you. There is nothing in my life more important than you, and yet I refuse to simply give in to that feeling.

What is it that makes me cry at every corny song, every TV show, every cheap movie about fathers and sons? There is a sadness buried deep inside of me. It's hard to see how I will ever be through with it. Perhaps through Dylan I will work it out.

From my grandfather to my father to me, and now perhaps to Dylan. This yearning for the perfect, warm, giving, loving, present father gets passed from generation to generation.

I focus too much on the negative. It has been much, much better between Dylan and me lately. It's proof that I really *can* change. And I will change more as time goes on. This is what matters the most. I'm not the perfect father. I'm not the perfect father. But I'm working on it, aware of it, struggling with it all the time. I would like to take time to talk with Michael about all this tomorrow. I hardly ever share these feelings with other fathers.

Would this feeling be as strong if Dylan were a girl? If he were a girl I don't think I'd be reliving so much of my own childhood. And I wouldn't have the responsibility of teaching him what it means to be a male, of being his role model. He takes in all of who I am. No amount of conscious effort changes that. He learns to be distant if I am distant, aggressive if I am aggressive. If I am unreliable, he learns not to trust men. It is a heavy burden, especially when I am aware of how much bullshit male programming I still carry around.

At least he doesn't learn to fuck women over, or to idolize them. And he learns that it's ok for men to be vulnerable, to hurt, to cry. It's not that I'm doing so badly. It's that he deserves more than I can possibly give him. We all deserve more than our fathers or mothers are able to give. That's what's so sad.

This sorrow is not guilt. It is, simply, sorrow. A huge reservoir of sadness. For me to admit how important Dylan is to me I must also admit how deeply I still want to be close to my father. That's a hard one.

Today I bought a card for Father's Day, a plain card on parchment paper that said inside: "For all the times I haven't said it...I love you." So simple. Can I say that so simply? Will he hear?

It's not too late to change, not too late to unravel the tangles, not too late to open my eyes, to my father as well as to my son.

That feels better. Now I can go on with the day. This has been time well spent.

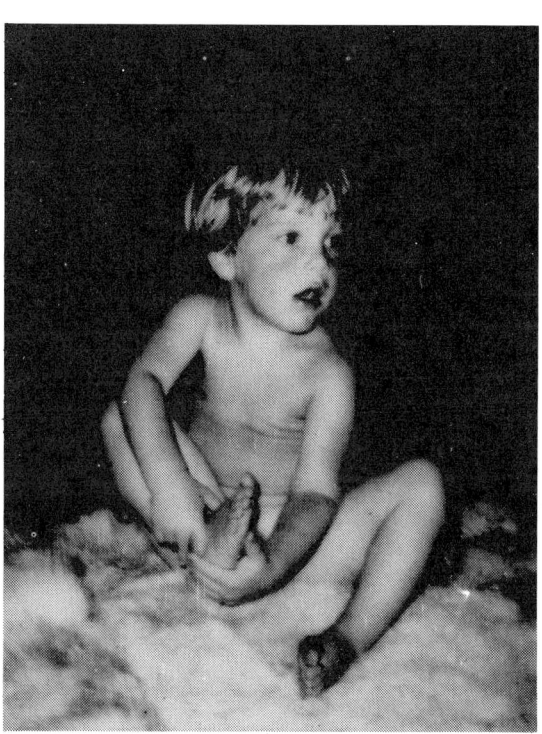

September, 1974: Susan begins to work full-time, getting a sudden and unexpected teaching job in place of day-to-day substituting. Susan is high and excited; it is the perfect job for her. I am less pleased. I remember the disruptions of full-time work and don't know how I will feel as a full-time parent and housekeeper. After an emotionally hard year, Susan and I are just coming together again. I am afraid the job will destroy all the new closeness, just as Dylan's birth uprooted our growing intimacy once before.

September 20, 1974

Mind out of focus. Dylan doesn't want to eat his chili, only his rolls and crackers. Shall we have a fight or should I let him carbohydrate himself to death? I am coming down with a cold.

September 26, 1974

Dylan tells me the story of Hansel and Gretel: "The boy eats the girl up because he doesn't like her." (!!) Also the story of the Three Little Pigs: "One pig oinks and goes to get another pig. Then two pigs are oinking. Then they go get another pig that oinks too. It's called Three Little Pigs and the pigs are building a house." It's amazing to see how he perceives things.

Later on he recounts how to write a capitol A: "First you go down, then the other way, then across." He draws in the air. To make a small a: "First you go around, then there's a little stop."

October 2, 1974

It's one thing to take care of Dylan half time, and something else entirely to be the one that's responsible for him day after day after day.

It's one thing to have time with Dylan while Susan's around. It's something else entirely to be stuck around the house every day with only a three-year-old for company.

Now I get to experience the life of the American mother and housewife. Already my days revolve around getting the housework done, doing errands, taking Dylan to and from play group. Once upon a time I told Susan this would be an interesting experiment, to see if I could enjoy keeping a clean house and being Dylan's most available parent. So far I'm not impressed.

December 7, 1974 (Saratoga)

Out for hot chocolate and English muffins with Dylan while Susan plays organ at a wedding. It is a bright, sunshiny, pre-Christmas Saturday, and this town is packed with cheery, well-to-do shoppers. I feel a little self-conscious here as Dylan spreads his set of counting cards over the counter, only to have the waitress gather them up as she serves our muffins. She says, "So you don't get jelly on them," but she means, "So you don't bother the other people by taking up too much space." I want to object but I am out of my territory and I don't want to make a fuss. I let it pass.

December 10, 1974

It's no wonder I have a hard time getting myself out of bed these mornings. This morning I went from the bedroom to the living room, letting my eyes gradually come into focus. The first thing I saw was that the dishes needed to be washed. Dishes from last night stacked by the sink, and Susan and Dylan's breakfast dishes out on the table. Dylan began insisting immediately that I read him a story. Out of bed five minutes and already behind on The Things That Need to Get Done. Ugh.

December 12, 1974

The sound of Dylan and Boogie laughing filters out through the closed door to Dylan's room. The sun brings its early morning slanting light into the kitchen...

Now Dylan and Boogie dance delicately to Bach organ fugues. The sun has risen above the redwoods and gushes in through the front window.

December 13, 1974

Yesterday I worked all day—cleaning, fixing the drip in the kitchen sink, repotting plants, baking bread. I was high with the feeling that at last I was getting on top of things.

Today I don't feel like doing anything at all. The more I try to regenerate yesterday's energy, the deeper I sink into the blahs. I went into the bathroom and discovered Dylan's muddy footprints and handprints all over the toilet and the sink. He had been in there with Susan and climbed up to wash his hands. I was mad at Susan for leaving another mess for me to clean up. I told her so, too. She made some comment about the bathroom being enough of a mess already that she didn't think it made much difference. I felt guilty (yes, I have been meaning to scour the bathroom but haven't gotten to it yet), stung by Susan's lack of understanding for how I feel being cooped up with housework and Dylan all the time, and angry at being criticized. I was feeling too much to say anything. I have been under a cloud all afternoon.

We are in the reverse of when I was working full-time. I wasn't very tuned in to Susan's difficulties then either.

December 15, 1974

Breakfast again with Dylan in Saratoga while Susan plays the organ. It is eight in the morning and the town is deserted. Coming into town from the hills was like entering a ghost town. Houses, stores, wide streets, no people.

I feel like Dylan and I are on the road. This is just the sort of place you always go to for breakfast when you're traveling. Formica counter, short-order cook, standard food, standard stools, Readiform checks. I fantasize taking a long trip with Dylan—stops at cafes, time in the car together, watching how different people respond to us as a traveling team. It would be fun, just him and me. Less lonely than traveling alone. Maybe in March or early April. It will be a true adventure. Dylan is getting to the age where we can expand the range of our sharing.

December 22, 1974 (Saratoga)

After two weeks at this coffee shop Dylan and I have already become an institution. The waitresses notice us when we come in, nod a familiar hello. The bright-eyed little boy and the father who sits and writes all the time. It feels nice to be part of the scene so quickly and easily. Are father-young-son pairs so rare? Or are we unusually picturesque?

January 18, 1975

Today I got mad at Dylan for leaving his toys around the house right after I had finished vacuuming and cleaning things up. Then I remembered my age-old contempt for parents who don't let their kids mess up their immaculate living rooms and I was totally embarrassed. Look at what I'm turning into, just from being a stay-at-home spouse! My self-esteem is bound to getting the house neat and clean, and that puts me up against Dylan's overflowing energy.

January 27, 1975

Dylan relates to Susan now like most kids do to their working fathers. Susan drives up and Dylan drops what he's doing to run out and greet her. He looks up at me with wide eyes and shouts excitedly, "Susan's home! Susan's come back!" If Susan is happy and rested they can have a wonderful playful time together in the evening. If Susan is tired or upset, Dylan clings and demands her attention and the house is filled with his threats and tantrums.

I'm kind of jealous of that special energy between Susan and Dylan. My own space with Dylan is so much less compressed and special. Mostly I wish I had less time with him rather than more.

What I do want is more time with Susan. Being around the house all day, sometimes not even speaking to another adult, is empty and lonely. I look forward to Susan coming home just so I'll have someone to talk to. When Susan walks in the door Dylan and I both jump for her. I don't want to compete with Dylan for her attention, to see which of us can push harder for what he wants.

We've talked about that a little, Dylan and I. I told him how I felt and asked him what he thought we could do to avoid that kind of fight. He told me that he never got to see Susan any more, to do things with her. Lying in bed together, snuggled up close, I didn't feel very competitive. It was true that he only saw Susan for a couple of hours before he went to bed whereas I had all evening with her. I agreed to respect the early evening as a time for him to mostly be with Susan, and to save my stories and demands until after he went to sleep. It feels like an important thing to have worked out between us directly, instead of through Susan.

February 7, 1975 (unfinished poem to Dylan)

> My son feels the dirt in the flowerpots, hoping that the
> plants need to be watered.
> My son checks the temperature by looking to see if the trees
> are dancing in the wind.
> My son says that Coriander the cat has told him he will
> stop eating the plants now.

My son wouldn't let Susan take his plant with her to school.

My son is afraid of clowns and roosters and getting stuck in the mud.

My son likes to climb under the covers with me and play that we're hiding from monsters.

My son likes to invite the monsters in for tea.

My son is even more impatient than I am, and always ready for a fight.

My son tells everyone in his play group what to do and gets upset if they won't do what he says.

My son would eat honey straight from the can if I let him.

My son carries on long conversations with the time lady.

My son mails books for me while I mail the letters.

My son runs the back end of the mimeograph while I run the front.

My son listens to records and tapes until he knows them word for word.

My son likes to burn honeysuckle incense above the fireplace.

My son's favorite colors are orange and pink, and sometimes purple.

My son likes to dance to a dozen different kinds of music.

My son likes to stir the flour into dough and level off the baking powder for pancakes.

My son asks his grandma why grandpa never cooks dinner.

February 8, 1975

Saturdays are terrible days. Dylan visits his demands on

Susan by whining and screaming and generally being obnoxious, which drives me up the wall and makes me want to just get up and leave. Often I feel that Susan doesn't even care or notice if Dylan's complaining upsets me. She just lets him go on and on, and when it's a fight between the two of them I don't feel that I should interfere. Susan is not as in tune with Dylan as I am these days. She just doesn't spend as much time with him. I could help her out, but I'm usually too mad at her to want to be helpful.

February 15, 1975

Reading Marge Piercy. Listening to Susan and Dylan go through their Saturday routine. He competes with me for Susan's attention, and Susan refuses to mediate. I do not want to play that triangular game, so I withdraw instead. No matter how much Susan knows that I hate Dylan's screaming and being unreasonable she will not cut him off. It makes me mad.

Maybe she just doesn't know *what* to do when he gets that way.

February 16, 1975

This morning I cut Dylan's hair too short. He doesn't mind. I don't mind either. Still, it's too short.

February 20, 1975

Dylan comes with me each week to work at the food co-op warehouse. He has become an institution there. He helps Lonnie prepare the price sheets. Louanne shows him how the adding machine works. Usually he finds a friendly volunteer and helps weigh out the fruits and vegetables. He knows more about co-op operations than most of the adult volunteers, so often he ends up telling adults what to do. It's fun watching how adults relate to being supervised by a four-year-old. Most people like working with him, and now that I've stopped worrying about him getting in people's ways I love it too.

It's a real pleasure to be able to take him to where I work. To have him share that part of my life. Our time together is best when we've got something to do. At the co-op he learns how to make his own way, how to deal with new people, how to make friends.

Afterwards we often go to the bar next door to unwind. I have a beer or two and write while he watches the people playing pool. It's a friendly, easy-going place. Sometimes people buy him peanuts or let him take a couple of shots on the pool table. He checks in with me from time to time, then goes off again on his own.

He's becoming his own person, making his own way through the world more and more without my help or interference.

March 3, 1975

It's 11:00 already. I have to write the publicity brochure for the co-op and get it down to Santa Cruz by 3:30. Tomorrow I reserve just to be with Dylan.

Today we rolled and tumbled in bed—joyfully, lightly. So nice to touch and laugh. The last time I saw my father he asked me if I remembered how we used to play mock football in bed. It's one of my fondest father-son memories. The times when touch was permitted. It's nice that he remembers that too.

I will pass my sensuality to Dylan, with all my strength, with all my grace. Amen.

March 19, 1975

Play group day. Boogie, Leifin, and Dylan as (respectively) superego, id, and ego. As parent, child, and adult.

Boogie seems unhappy to me today. He and Dylan were fine by themselves but when Leifin came Boogie started whining a lot and doing things to make other people see how important he was.

Actually they've all been fine today; it's just me that's in a bad mood. One hour to go. I am surviving this day. Then Jim will come for Leifin, Mary for Boogie. Susan will come home from school.

The kids threaten to come back in from outside. What to do if they come in? I'll break out brownies and milk and we'll have a party. There. I am protected from their assault, taking care of myself. Hooray! Sometimes I forget that self-protection is as basic a need as love, touch, and food.

March 22, 1975

I am really dependent on Dylan these days for emotional companionship. His is the realest relationship in my life right now. That's a heavy burden to lay on his shoulders, and I want to be careful about that. Maybe I have been reluctant to pursue nursery schools because I know I'll miss his company. I should take a second look at all that. Nursery school would open up a whole new world for Dylan, and would give me more free time as well. Why have I resisted? I've been clinging to Dylan's company without being the least bit aware of what I was doing.

March 29, 1975

A family day. We left Berkeley this morning so we could

have time to stop at the Oakland Museum and let Dylan trip out on all the stuffed animals and memorabilia from California history. He loved the animal displays, the old fire engines, the preserved insects. Here we are, a family on vacation together.

I'm looking forward to driving cross-country with Dylan and Susan this summer. A good way for us to come together again after a long year. It will be fun to watch Dylan's reactions to different things, different places, different people. A chance to see the world through his eyes.

Dylan plays in the 55-gallon drums this playground has converted into tunnels, climbs the geodesic monkey bars and the cyclone fence, asks me to swing him, accepts my writing as good reason for my not obliging. Susan practices the organ.

Dylan is delightful today—bright sunshine energy, lots of curiosity, exploration, and confidence. It makes me feel good to be with him.

> Bright light,
> you dissipate the shadowy museum quiet
> as you gobble up the scenes and sights.
> You turn this delicately preserved theatre
> into a colossal playground wonderland.
> Others greet you with surprise and pleasure,
> I with a quiet glow
> rich as my love
> of this exciting, adventuring,
> most totally alive
> you.

> You are a lens for me.
> You show me the crystal magic
> of each little moment, each detail
> that so easily passes beneath notice
> into ordinary reality.

I remember:
I too played unwitting prism
for my parents' world.
It is the free gift of children
that balances the care and attention of parents—
offerings exchanged without purpose.

April 10, 1975

Parents meeting of Dylan's nursery school. Middle-class house with proper furnishings, proper refreshments, proper people. Mothers and mothers and mothers and me.

I decided to take Dylan along since I couldn't get a baby sitter and he said he wanted to go. After all, it's *his* school. He said he would just fall asleep in my lap. He didn't. I ended up holding him while he tried to sleep, squirming and obviously uncomfortable the whole time. Stares and "poor you" offers of advice from various mothers. I thought I'd die. I tried to be cool. Oh, look how awkward and strange men are with children! I was too embarrassed to get out of my armchair and sit on the floor where Dylan would have more room.

Never again. Never again.

April 11, 1975

Good talking with Lane this morning about kids and schools. Her positive words about Dylan meant a lot to me, especially after last night's fiasco. Lane says she finds Dylan very mellow and uncompetitive. Her perspective helps me feel good about Dylan and then good about me as a father. Fathering is something I do well after all. It's not a marketable skill, but it's an important one to me.

April 17, 1975

Eight in the morning and already I'm in a tizzy. Dylan fusses about having a cookie before breakfast, the 18th round of a boring and debilitating fight. I get mad at him and finally put him in his room. Susan is looking at me as if to say I'm a madman.

What's going on with me? Every time I think I've got a handle on life, everything unravels. Usually I manage to keep it all together. Why is it so difficult now?

I feel incompetent, unable to take charge of my life. Then I feel silly for being so weak, so filled with self-pity. I resolve to be strong, but that too collapses. I am defeated, a failure, undisciplined.

When Susan asks how my day was I say fine, wondering why I'm saying fine when I have been grouchy and irritable and fighting with Dylan all day. I guess I feel that if I put that stuff out to her I'll push her further away. At the end of the day I'm usually anxious to just feel close again.

There's another part too. It's hard for me to admit that I'm not doing something well. It's like at the nursery school meeting when everything was falling apart. No matter what, I tried to keep a stiff upper lip. Oh no, I can handle it, thank you. What a garbage cycle!

What do I need? I feel like I need to re-center myself. Maybe what I *really* need is to let myself fall apart.

Dylan interrupts and we have a fight about whether a picture in Newsweek is of real or toy cars.

Fuck it! I'm going to have breakfast.

April 19, 1975

Dylan wants me to write about him. What shall I write? I

read as I write, word for word. He sits and watches me. Now he wants me to say something in particular—that his grandma and grandpa should have a happy birthday.

Dylan and Susan decide to make waffles together. Dylan brings in a carton of eggs from the refrigerator. He struggles to crack an egg, every bit of his attention focused on what he's doing. Susan and I share an appreciative smile.

(later, Saratoga)

Dylan says loudly, "Doesn't that man eat like a monkey?"
"Dylan!" I chide, embarrassed.

"No, really," he insists, pointing. "I've seen monkeys eat like that." He imitates the man. I laugh with him. The truth is that I had just noticed how strangely that man was devouring his ice cream, though I hadn't thought of a monkey. I avoid looking to see if the man is listening to us. Then I take a quick glance over my shoulder. It's true, he looks a lot like a monkey—lips out, eating fast, excitedly. I swallow my embarrassment. Sorry, people, I'm not going to squash Dylan's interest in the world for your comfort, or for mine.

April 29, 1975 (bus trip to Albion)

Early morning start for this excursion. We ride to Santa Cruz with Susan at 8:00. The bus doesn't leave till 9:30. We buy tickets, walk around, get coffee. We read the bus schedule as we sit. I explain how to read up for Santa Cruz to San Francisco, down for San Francisco to Santa Cruz. We trace the route of the bus we will take.

On the bus finally. Dylan looks at his books (good planning, David) as I write. We keep our bags with us. We are a self-contained unit, the two of us. Whatever we need for this week is right here under the seat. Small enough to carry short distances and big enough to include books and toys for Dylan.

Dylan is down on the floor, checking everything he can find out about the bus. He discovers the adjustable foot rest. Click, click, click, down.

Saratoga. Dylan hustles orange slices from the woman in the back seat. I wonder if that's ok with her, decide it's between the two of them.

Cupertino. Dylan staggers down the aisle to the bathroom. He says he wants to wash his hands. The bathroom is occupied. Then it's free. He disappears inside. I wait and watch as the bus lurches, stops, starts. I reassure myself that he can't hurt himself badly in the bathroom of a bus. Still, what's taking him so long? Finally he comes out again, pushes the door closed, goes back, shuts it tight, comes back to the seat. Another successful voyage out alone.

San Francisco. Dylan sleeps standing up, folded at the waist onto the seat. If I move him he'll wake for sure. I leave him standing. We'll be getting off the bus in a few minutes anyway.

Switch buses, walk around downtown San Francisco, wait on line, start the second leg of the journey.

Petaluma. Dylan sits on the floor, lost in talk and self-amusement. I'm enjoying writing these random notes. Now Dylan disappears completely under the seat in front of us.

Cloverdale. Dylan is still enjoying himself. I tell him it's an hour and a half to Albion. He says cheerfully that he can wait that long, that it will be fun to ride on a windy road over the mountains. Who could ask for a more enjoyable traveling companion?

May 2, 1975 (Albion)

> Lovely, loving bath with Dylan
> warmth of water and warmth of boy
> washing my soul with my back
>   my feet, my penis
> loving careful careless caresses
> softening me a little at a time
> until I melt into evening's fading light.
>
> Now I look into the bedroom
> and find a contented sleeping boy
>   peace incarnate
> with red cheeks and blue sleeper.
> I turn the electric blanket down
> and feel my heart rush into my throat.

May 13, 1975

    Santa Cruz library. A woman holds her daughter on her lap and leisurely reads her a story. The girl sucks her thumb and holds onto a rag doll. Dylan picks out a book. He listens to the mother reading the story. He picks up his book, goes over, and listens some more. The woman is reading to her daughter about tanks and soldiers shooting each other. Come on, Dylan, we've got better things to do.

July 31, 1975 (Milford, Pa., visiting my parents)

Feeling far away. Dylan fusses and screams and carries on. I find myself furious, then withdrawn.

Dylan does everything he can to attack me, and I sit and take it because I don't want to make more distance between us. Susan explains that this is how four-year-olds are, which makes no difference to me. It is hard, painful, to feel him pushing me away all the time.

Dylan screams again. A physical discharge sweeps from my head down over my shoulders. I feel rageful towards him. I imagine slapping him across the face, hard. Grabbing him by the arm and throwing him to the ground.

Dylan screams more. Susan threatens to spank him. Two rounds later she actually does spank him once. Now he's crying about that and I'm going to take a shower and drown out the noise.

> Vacuum.
> The top of the head lifts off,
> there is nothing underneath.
> All motion ceases.
> All thought fades into the distance.
> Nothing remains.

August 1, 1975 (Milford)

> Voices drift up the stairs:
> a grandfather's dramatic reading,
> a four-year-old's receptive delight.
> The rest is quiet.
> Susan has gone down to say good morning.
> I lie here a little longer,

semen drying on my softened skin,
listening,
enjoying the observer's distance,
not needing to do anything more
than absorb the color of the sunlight.

August 16, 1975

Dylan sleeps softly
behind the bars of his new loft
breathing deeply
arm outstretched
surrounded by the scent
of new-cut wood.

I have worked three days
to fashion this nest,
special bed to soften the chill
of sleeping alone.
He has felt the love in my work
and I have felt his growing excitement.
Through the sawing and the hammering,
the drilling and the sanding,
we have touched close again.

* * * * * *

The books say it is a stage:
that all four-year-old sons
push their fathers away
with icy efficiency.
    So what?
My mind understands

      rationalizes
      repairs
      consoles
but I have opened my heart
and the wounds bleed real blood
day after day after day.

I am embarrassed to be so vulnerable
to one who is so small.
But there is a voice in me
as young as you
that misses your special love
and shivers at the space between us.
I wait
and lick wounds
and remember that change comes
in its own time.
For now I notice:
the more I recognize the four-year-old in me
the more I love four-year-old you.

August 18, 1975

     Corelli and Pachelbel take turns soothing me, drawing me out. I am flooded with energy, and thoughts about how much I hold back, still, from the fullness of being a father. I am scared by the strength of my feelings. The warning that rattles around inside is: "If I go into all that I will lose myself entirely." Lose myself or find myself. I wonder which.

     My resistance has to do with being taken advantage of. I enjoy taking care of Dylan, taking care of Susan too, but I don't want to have to do it all the time. To avoid being swamped I cut off my positive feelings about taking care of someone else. Then I feel selfish, withdrawn, cut off.

September 6, 1975 (Albion)

Foghorns deep in the night. High and low moans filling the silence with far-away, empty, lonely sounds. Dylan is enjoying himself here, adapting easily to the new situation, playing well with the other children or by himself, or moving with me. I enjoy his company, enjoy helping him out, watching him get oriented to this new place. He does well and I get a feeling of confidence and inner strength from him. It is a good, warm, confirming feeling. I feel close to him and feel him being close to me.

I'm glad he decided to come, glad for his energy, his presence, his delight—as today unloading firewood from the truck, or tonight singing songs and playing drums while Peter played piano.

Now we curl together on this mattress, sleeping in a tipi for the first time. We gather little pieces of wood, build a little fire to keep warm, light two candles for light. I read him a bedtime story, the two of us stretched out side by side on our bellies. I tell him I am going to write but that he should go to sleep. He agrees. He likes the togetherness as much as I do. He snuggles into his sleeping bag, laid out next to mine, rustles around a little, and waits for sleep to come. I write and look over at him from time to time. He grins at me. I grin back. My heart melts. Then he is asleep, secure as can be. A very warm, fatherly feeling to wrap up in before going to sleep.

Blow out the candles, listen to the foghorns, and float away.

September 8, 1975 (Albion)

> Lonely.
> The feeling is lonely in a roomful of people.
> Only Dylan provides company.
> We retreat to the porch.
> I shift, center.

Lonely dissolves into a peaceful myself place,
watching the fog,
smelling the first fog breezes.
Look, Dylan!
The sliveriest sliver of a moon.

September 24, 1975

Dylan similes: as nice as a warm day when no one in the whole world is doing anything mean; as tight as a very big turtle with a very small shell.

October 1, 1975

Dylan has been coughing for two hours, unable to go to sleep. So I'm sitting in his room, trying to cool him out enough so that he can drop off. I'm frustrated, powerless, tense, angry. I have created this evening time only to have it consumed by the irritation of hearing Dylan cough himself silly. I have tried cough medicine, orange juice, brandy, vaporizer. I don't know what else to do. He seems to cough less with me here, so I'll just sit here a while. I want to run away, if I only knew where to run *to*. I don't. Sshhh. Dylan is asleep. Thank God.

There is more to do than I can possibly manage. Dylan coughs again. Jesus! I take the record off, hoping to encourage him to go back to sleep. He stops coughing again. I am exhausted.

October 5, 1975

Seven times
    they made me say it seven times.

Seven times
> "I have a four-year-old
> who fell down some stairs."

Seven times
> "He doesn't seem to be hearing well
> this morning."

Seven times
> remembering that bureaucracy is an attempt
> to make hospitals efficient.

Seven times
> keeping my voice as flat as hers.

Seven times
> waiting through the click, the pause,
> the new person introducing herself.

Seven times
> wanting to hang up and hide.

Then an hour's wait
before meeting the doctor,
> the deserted office making our voices
> and footsteps into echoes,

all to clear two little ears
of long-gathering wax
and open me to soaking up
every drop
of a very ordinary
> Sunday morning.

This morning was frightening, terrifying. I have yet to discharge the energy. Asking Dylan questions he couldn't hear.

Such a contrast to his usual alert self. I kept up a good front for Dylan's sake (?!), and felt my heart crumble inside.

"Dylan can you hear me?" Talking low. He goes on without

responding.

I hold my breath and push inside my chest. Louder: "Dylan, how is your ear?"

"Huh?"

Aargh. I must avoid panic. I do and I don't.

I call Kaiser Hospital, get passed from operator to operator to nurse. The same at Dominican, where I am finally told to call my own doctor before bothering the hospital. Yes, but don't you see, I'm very scared...

Oh, Dylan, it would be terrible to see your total absorption cut off by an accidental tumble, a clunk on the head. And through it all he is so completely innocent and trusting. Sitting on the floor I clutch him to me, my arms tight around his little legs, just to be close to him.

October 7, 1975

I pick up Dylan at nursery school and we go to see if Leifin wants to come visit this afternoon. He does. Lane's baby was due yesterday. She watches Dylan intently.

I make quesadillas while Dylan gets used to having Leifin here and Leifin figures out how to deal with Dylan bossing him around. With play group in disarray it's been quite a while since they've spent time together. Leifin gets belligerent, then coy, in response to being overwhelmed. Dylan wants to make it clear that he's in charge here. Marsha was telling me that Dylan took charge of the whole nursery school when they played dominoes. I believe it.

October 9, 1975

Tonight I feel unexpectedly content. Before Dylan went to

bed we took a moment just to be together, lying quietly on the floor. I loved the time, did my usual wondering about why I don't take this kind of time with Dylan more often. But tonight I notice the change that is represented by my taking this kind of time at all. I see these spaces growing longer and more frequent over time.

There has been a real change this year. I no longer see myself as second parent to Susan. I've had time to learn about being the person most responsible for Dylan, to get to like myself in that role, to feel good about myself as a father. I got dragged into that place kicking and screaming, but I'm glad for the changes that have resulted.

November 26, 1975

It is fine to raise Dylan righteously, but sometimes I wonder if we aren't creating a gulf between him and other kids. Today Dylan and I looked for someone to come over and play. Dylan just wanted to have a visitor. Leifin wanted to stay home. Boo wanted to stay home. Jason wanted to stay home. Is there something about me and Dylan that everyone finds strange? Do they expect some kind of mothering that I don't give? Or is Dylan just more adventurous and confident than the other four-year-olds?

Yesterday Jason said he would come visit, but when we went to pick him up he got all shy and said he wanted to stay home instead. Dylan was really looking forward to the afternoon. He burst into tears when Jason's mother said he could stay home if he wanted to.

November 29, 1975

Something about this year, something about Dylan becoming

old enough to understand, something about the onslaught of Christmas, is making me feel very Jewish. It's strange since I haven't felt very Jewish for years and years and years. But this evening I am really enjoying the chanukkah candles on the table, the idea that we have actually started lighting chanukkah candles, and that Dylan enjoys it.

November 30, 1975

> The plainest menorah
> and wrong
> cut hurriedly from scrap redwood trim
> for an almost forgotten chanukkah
> two years ago.
> I did not know the shammash
> should be in the center
> and it looked better
> over on one side.
> The candles will set the whole thing on fire
> as we discovered the first year,
> so now we put little squares of aluminum foil
> over the charred holes.
> And only this third year did I think
> to oil the wood
> and erase "bathroom door" from the bottom
> where the trim was to have been put.
>
> It was because Dylan was two
> that I resurrected this celebration
> from the attic of my childhood,
> adding even the prayer,
> in butchered Hebrew,
> that Malcolm learned once upon a time

as a boy in Tucson.
Now amidst the Christmas music
and the street decorations
and the shopping
and the Santa Clauses
and the trees
and the stockings
and the gingerbread houses
and the greeting cards
each night the candles burn quietly for one hour
building slowly to a silent climax
in alternative ritual.
There is no need for more—
I am content with this statement
and Dylan's usually unspoken sense
that it feels right for these candles
to take us from day to night
these few days.

December 2, 1975

Dylan and I come to Dean's cafe for grilled cheese sandwiches and milk. Dylan is really irritating me. This is our only time together today and I would like to enjoy it, but all he can think about is Trelawny's birthday party and how long it is until 3:00. It's as if the present doesn't even exist for him.

This is turning into a bum day. I want to sleep.

December 3, 1975

Yesterday was a total disaster. Fighting with Dylan forever, it seemed, about the stupid birthday party. I yelled at him, I told him I was tired and not feeling good and needed for him to be nice to me, but all he would do is complain and complain about how long it was until the party. Finally I told him that if he wasn't nice to me, I wasn't going to be nice to him either, that I wouldn't drive him to the party and he'd have to stay home. It was an idle threat, but I was mad. I watched his face crumble at the thought of not being able to go to the party. I was sorry I had said it. It was a low blow. I told him I would take him but I wanted to sleep until five minutes to three. Then I got into bed and actually went to sleep.

Sometimes it's like I give and I give and I give but I'm not allowed to ask for anything in return. He's only four and a half, after all, and much too preoccupied with his own world to spend very much time making sacrifices for me. It's all so one-sided, it doesn't seem fair. Yesterday I just wanted him to understand that I needed some special attention, and there was no way to communicate that to him.

December 4, 1975

> I feel pain at every failure,
> every loving moment denied,
> every missed possibility,
> every wisdom not yet perfected.
> So much is needed
> and I know how to give so little.
> Dig a hole in the sand,
> try to trap the ocean.
>
> Where are all the moments of utter openness?
> Some times are so incredibly beautiful
> it is hard to accept the others.
> The angel of light comes and goes.

I mourn every time she leaves.
Dig a hole in the sand,
try to trap the ocean.

December 11, 1975

Nine o'clock and barely awake. I have a schedule that squeezes in an hour's work today but leaves no time for breakfast. Tomorrow is a day to share with Susan, then Saturday to San Jose to find a violin for Dylan and cut a Christmas tree. I haven't thought about what to say when I speak at Glenn's class tonight...

The trouble with getting my life together is that I begin to expect it to stay that way. Of course, it immediately falls apart...

December 14, 1975

This morning I'm mad at Susan, and at Dylan too. Susan is pissed off because I didn't get up with Dylan so she could sleep late in peace.

What happened was that Dylan came in, wanting someone to get up with him. I told him I'd get up, but he insisted that he wanted to be with Susan. I thought that was a pain, but I wasn't going to fight him about it. I left it for him and Susan to work out. Susan says that if I'd just gotten up Dylan would have stopped insisting on being with her. I suppose that's true, and if she had said that when we were in bed I would have gotten up. But I didn't think of it. How am I supposed to know what she wants if she doesn't tell me?

December 17, 1975

Tonight I took Dylan with me to men's group. I explained

that Susan and I have a Wednesday night conflict and that I'd like to try bringing Dylan regularly and see how that worked out. Everyone felt fine about that.

There is something right about bringing Dylan to the men's group. Some connection between my changes in this group and my changes from being with Dylan. The softening, the gradual learning to love and be loved, the letting go of trying so hard, the making room for warmth and contact. Being in this group of warm, appreciative, loving men has helped me open to Dylan, and being with Dylan has prepared me for new openness with men. Through both I am melted into a new way of being in the world. Call it the yinning of David. I feel like I'm becoming whole.

December 18, 1975

An old-fashioned Thursday night alone. I'm edgy. Hungry but I can't find anything I want to eat. Dishes wait to be washed, packages to wrap and put under the Christmas tree.

Dylan coughs in his sleep, sick again. There is too much to deal with; I am inadequate to the task. It's an old feeling come back to haunt me again. Maybe I should let myself get sick and let it all go. Give up. Let the food co-op disorganize itself. Huddle in the security of a warm bath. Visit people in San Francisco and forget about Boulder Creek. Run away to...anywhere.

Never give up without a fight! Be more loving to Susan when she gets home. Get into Dylan's violin trip tomorrow and Susan's faculty dinner party afterwards. Do this, do that.

I hate this overwhelmed feeling. I feel it less than I used to but it still reaches up and grabs me sometimes. It is the solstice, the bottom of the darkness. This too will pass. I will look back on this week with understanding and paternal warmth.

Enough of this bullshit. Go do the dishes already.

December 19, 1975

I am refusing to cop to Christmas this year, to care about it more than I do. "It's not my holiday" keeps running through my mind. Dyaln feels my resistance, but mostly he's into it.

"What Christmas is about is Jesus being born," Dylan says. Well, no. Well, yes, but it's more... How can I explain to a four-year-old why it upsets me that a month of every year is devoted to Christmas shopping?

Bob Stern doesn't show up for Dylan's first violin lesson. Dylan is crushed. Weeks of anticipation and excitement leading up to a big zero in the rain. I don't know what to say. Bob leaves a note saying he's sorry, that he tried to reach us. I comfort Dylan as best as I can, then we go out for hot cider and cheese sticks to recuperate. I hate to use food for comfort, but just this once... We watch the Santa Cruz people and wait for Susan. Dylan feels better.

January 4, 1976

Susan and Dylan have been gone four days, visiting Susan's parents. It has been a good week for me, hard but fruitful. Now I get ready for them to come back.

By the last day of alone I begin to find the rhythm of alone. It has been a phoenix time, falling through the bottom to find the top. I am ready to be together again, energy high for reunion.

There is another feeling too. I do not want this clarity, this opening born in these days alone, to be taken away. The rush of Dylan's energy leaves little room for slow settling. I see two lives: this place alone, and another balancing spirit with Dylan. I move between the two, each in its time.

Smiles and doubts, the vision and the anticipation. This is the mantra born of these four days of fruitful struggle.

January 12, 1976

Boogie comes for play group and Dylan shows him all his new Christmas toys. He shows Boogie how they work, then delights in watching Boogie throw Magicdarts and play with his toy bowling set. It's fun to watch Dylan be so charming. He is growing up into a regular boy. Boogie shoots the bowling game, Dylan rolls the balls back down the ball return. Boogie throws the darts, Dylan counts up the score.

Leifin comes. Three is harder than two. Now it is constant hassling. I give them peanut butter and jelly sandwiches. Maybe it's just that they're hungry. It doesn't seem to make much difference.

Dylan and Leifin have a fight about the bowling game. Dylan argues, Leifin pushes him aside. In the end, Dylan wins. Now Leifin gets to be shooter. Boogie goes off to do something else. Leifin takes the balls and runs away. Dylan tells him he's supposed to use the shooter. The game disintegrates.

Hot orange curry warms my body from within. A cool breeze feels good coming in the front door. Boogie and Leifin set up the Sesame Street game. Dylan goes off with his tape recorder. Tranquility returns.

January 15, 1976

Watching Dylan, appreciating how well he seems to have survived the first years of his life. For the most part his spirit is intact. Slowly he is building his sense of himself, which he can then use to combat all the influences that would break him down. I think of Felice's remark about letting children go to public school only after they've gotten their shit detectors working. Dylan's seems to be working pretty well. Shall we send him to public school next year? Or what?

January 22, 1976

Bright late afternoon sun squints my eyes. Dylan throws stale bread to seagulls and ducks. "A coot got that one," he says. Now a herd follows him around—coots, mallards, gulls—as he stamps dry crusts into little pieces of food. He looks like a preacher up there on the hill, addressing his flock of attentive gulls.

A girl comes and scares the gulls away. Dylan offers her bread to feed the ducks that remain. Soon she has to go. A hundred birds are gathered around him and his bag full of old bread. "I hope a gull doesn't land in my bag," he says.

Another girl comes, takes Dylan's bag, and dumps out the last bunch of bread with a triumphant laugh. Dylan laughs too. "It's all done," he says. He asks if we have time to stay a while longer.

We move to the playground—Dylan to the turning wheel, me to the top of the little knoll. He climbs to the center of the wheel as it spins, alert and confident, talking to all the other kids. He is becoming very much a five-year-old. I am inspired by his clarity and his confidence. I feel good, sitting here after a day at the co-op, having no further commitments, just watching him.

Today he learned how to run a mimeograph machine. The co-op bought a new machine and the salesman came to show people how to use it. Dylan was fascinated. More information to fit into his head.

His hair is definitely turning brown. I feel sorry somehow. The child I have known is a blond. I'm glad the change is gradual, it gives me time to get used to it. What will he look like with black hair?

Dylan climbs the spiral slide. It's a struggle going up the down way but he makes it to the top. Another conquest. He is pleased with himself. He slides back down.

Time to start heading home. Get gas, check the post office box, call Marilyn to see if she can take Dylan to play group tomorrow. I offer Dylan one more slide before we go, accept his counter-offer of two. A man is playing classical guitar on the bench while his lady sits with her arms around her knees. I let the music come to me while Dylan finishes his two slides.

February 4, 1976

Dylan has settled into the men's group routine. He plays with people as we gather, then snuggles into his sleeping bag and gets quiet when the meeting starts. Usually he reads a while, then listens a while, then falls asleep. I think he likes the idea of coming to the men's group. Another part of my adult life that he can share, or maybe there's something special about being one of the men. I like the feeling of him joining this group of gentle men. I am teaching my son what it means to be a warm, loving, open man.

Tonight I told the men in the group that I won't be needing to bring Dylan to meetings any more. They seemed disappointed that they wouldn't get to see him. Maybe I should just keep bringing him.

March 8, 1976

I am enjoying this day, just being here in the present again. Something is going on in me, something about giving up the quest.

My path seems more yin than the paths of other men I know —more indirect, more unintentional. I see it in the poetry, in the spontaneous times, in the ability to listen, to see, to take in what's around me. My accomplishments have to do with being a father, a husband, a friend, rather than being a published writer. More and more that is becoming enough for me.

Dylan sits and reads. Leifin builds an elaborate machine with connector blocks. Dylan looks up, impressed with Leifin's creation.

"Say! How did you make that?"

"I just made it. I made it for you."

"I don't want it."

"What do you want? A gun?"

"I don't want anything."

Dylan goes back to his book—very present, very clear. Leifin goes back to his project without trying to hold onto Dylan's attention. It is an afternoon of deep peace. A time of blessing.

March 18, 1976

Dylan has gotten a fat envelope from his Grandpa Bert, full of stamps. Old ones too. Now we really will have to buy an album.

Rediscovering stamps with Dylan has been a real joy for me. Something I love to do, something for me and Dylan to share, something from my own childhood. We work together soaking stamps off of envelopes, drying them on paper towels, arranging them in the book we bought in Santa Cruz. The day we bought it I called it Dylan's book, but he corrected me. "It's yours too, of course," he said seriously. It's important to him that this is something I like to do, not just something I do for his sake.

It's the same as when he helps me put out mailings to publicize *Yellow Brick Road*. He puts the flyers in envelopes, sorts the envelopes by zip codes, while I type addresses. He loves participating in my life, and I love the sense of us working together.

It flashes me back to when I was a kid, helping my father address copies of the life insurance newsletter he edited. I loved being part of his work life, the work that was usually separate from me. And I loved being useful and competent. My mother helped too—it was a family project, a context for being together.

Now I live out those feelings from the other side. It is a very deep, warm feeling. A completion. And it builds yet another connection between Dylan and me.

March 21, 1976

Dream from last night: Somehow I know that Dylan is about to give birth. It's strange because he's so small, but I feel that it's ready to happen and I don't know what to do. I call my childhood family doctor to get his advice. He's skeptical. He asks how I know that Dylan is going to give birth. I remember for the first time that Dylan is a boy—boys don't give birth. I can't prove to the doctor that it's going to happen. I will have to handle it on my own.

March 23, 1976

I snuggle into the sleeping bag on the couch, where I have spent the night listening for Dylan's breathing after he woke up with another case of croup. It is warm and soft in this cocoon. I like it here. Dylan and Susan play cards together and let me write in peace. Thank you.

Let the past go and come to the present.

Let it go, let it flow,
everything, everything,
everything goes.

Susan and Dylan finish their game. Susan goes to dry her hair. Dylan asks if he can come up on the couch.

"No," I say quietly.

"Why not?"

"Because I want to be by myself."

He pauses.

"Why do you want to be by yourself?"

"I just like to be by myself sometimes."

Satisfied, he leaves. I think it's good to teach him that it's ok for me to be alone sometimes, so he doesn't feel that I'm rejecting him personally. He comes back as I write that.

"We're going to the movies at 3:30."

"Yes." I don't look up.

"When are we going to leave?"

"Dylan, I don't want to talk about that. I'm writing."

"But when are we going to leave?"

"I don't want to talk to you."

He cries once, then goes into his room, gets a book and comes back to read while I write—both of us sitting on the couch. Once again, a clear exchange. But my chest is tight with his interruption. Interruption of what? When the river curves around a hill, is that an interruption or the shape of its bed? I breathe and take the time to include Dylan in my flow.

March 29, 1976

A day of puttering around putters into evening. I have been alone most of the day, with low energy. I realize that I would rather have been with Dylan.

I have the sense of beauty fading with the sunset. I cry for the beauty, the beauty that comes and goes. It comes more often these days, as I open more and more. I cry now the way I cried when I first saw how much Dylan meant to me, lying in front of the fireplace, unable to pretend any longer that he was less than a vital part of my life.

I feel that with Susan too these days. That big heavy door opening, that possibility, that vulnerability. Dylan has opened me to a new level of loving, something I have been able to share with him that I hadn't allowed with anyone else.

It's the same message that hit me one evening, sitting in the candlelight, listening to Pachelbel. The difficulty of letting the simple beauty in, the fear of getting hurt, the pull against being open, being free. It is hard to let the beauty in when I am afraid it will go away and leave me way out on a limb. That is the risk— with Dylan, with Susan, with anyone else.

How can there be so much? Why me? Will it vanish tomorrow? In a week? In a season? Slowly I am learning to let myself feel what I feel, to stop holding back so much of who I am. I am growing. I am coming alive. I am being born.

I LOVE YOU
DYLAN

Other books by David Steinberg:

Yellow Brick Road: steps toward a new way of life, co-edited with Ann Dilworth. A collection of narratives, songs, poems and letters exploring alternative approaches to work, family, marriage, sexuality, community, birth and death—all focusing on the personal experiences of the contributors. 174 pages, 6" x 9", illustrated, perfectbound, $2.95.

Welcome, Brothers: poems of a changing man's consciousness. A collection of poems about trust and sharing among men, fathering, men's groups, surrender, and change. 32 pages, 8½" x 5½", illustrated, saddle-stitched, $1.50.

If I Knew the Way . . . (poems), 24 pages, 8½" x 5½", saddle-stitched, $1.00.

These books may be ordered from Red Alder Books, Box 545, Ben Lomond, CA 95005. Please include 50 cents extra for postage and handling.

Books from Times Change Press

FOR MEN AGAINST SEXISM: A Book of Readings—Edited by Jon Snodgrass. Men profoundly influenced by feminism analyze and share personal experiences of male sexuality and socialization, recent actions to combat sexism, and the special oppressions of Third World, working class and gay men. These men's goal: to transform themselves and revolutionize patriarchal society. *240 pp; $6.00.*

THE GREAT HARMONY: Teachings and Observations of the Way of the Universe—Edited by S. Negrin. This collection of teachings, drawn from Taoism, Western philosophy, "primitive" religions, Judaism, Zen and more, tells us that the sensory world is not an end in itself, but a path to knowledge. Understanding the laws of the universe is possible and leads to an artful life and ultimate self-realization. These teachings help illuminate the path. *128 pp; $3.50.*

HELLO, I LOVE YOU! Voices from within the Sexual Revolution—Edited by Jeanne pasle-green and Jim Haynes. Forty-eight pioneer-participants in the ongoing sexual revolution share their intimate, firsthand experiences with bisexuality, celibacy, erotic art, group sex, sado-masochism, gay and women's liberation. Here we have people taking risks to become more open and loving in a conscious search for better ways for us all to relate to ourselves and each other. *176 pp; $4.50.*

FATHERJOURNAL: Five Years of Awakening to Fatherhood—David Steinberg. This is a sensitive, unglorified account of a father who decides not to become "the second, somewhat foreign parent." Instead, he seeks intimate, nurturing contact with his child, and reveals for us the resulting emotional and sex-role conflicts, as well as the new levels of love and awareness that fatherhood opens to him. *96 pp; $3.00.*

FREE SPACE: A Perspective on the Small Group in Women's Liberation—Pamela Allen. *Free Space* is a good handbook for people wondering how to begin or restructure a consciousness-raising group. Developed by feminists, the small group is now being used by many people as a way of relating to different needs. *Illustrated; 64 pp;$2.00.*

JANUARY THAW: People at Blue Mt. Ranch Write About Living Together in the Mountains. Writing about relationships, work, parents, children, healing and celebration, these rural communards describe feeling their way toward a life that makes sense and feels good, in which people are more in harmony with themselves, each other, the earth and the universe. *Illustrated; 160 pp; $3.25. Cloth, $8.50.*

THE EARLY HOMOSEXUAL RIGHTS MOVEMENT (1864-1935)—John Lauritsen and David Thorstad. The gay movement, like the women's movement, has an early history, which, beginning in 1864, advanced the cause of gay rights until the 1930s when Stalinist and Nazi repression obliterated virtually all traces of it. The authors uncover this history, highlighting interesting people and events. *Illustrated; 96 pp; $2.75. Cloth, $6.95.*

MOMMA: A Start on All the Untold Stories—Alta. This is Alta's intensely personal story of her life with her two young daughters, and her struggle to be a writer. She tells of her efforts toward self-fulfillment and her battle against feelings of guilt—a story many readers will recognize as their own. *Illustrated; 80 pp;$2.25.*

AMAZON EXPEDITION: A Lesbianfeminist Anthology—Edited by Phyllis Birkby, Bertha Harris, Jill Johnston, Esther Newton and Jane O'Wyatt. When lesbians within the gay liberation movement synthesized gay politics with feminism, they started a separate political/cultural development which thousands of women began to identify with. This is what this anthology is about. Culture, herstory, politics, celebration. Lesbianfeminism—one concept: the new womanity. *Illustrated; 96 pp; $3.00. Cloth, $6.50.*

LISTEN TO THE MOCKING BIRD: Satiric Songs To Tunes You Know—Tuli Kupferberg. Radical songs can't make the new world, but they can help. And they can help you endure this one. Especially if they're humorous. Over 50 songs to delight and thrill you and yes make you laugh. *Illustrated; 64 pp; $1.50.*

THIS WOMAN: Poetry of Love and Change—Barbara O'Mary. This journal tells of a year of intense change—involving Barbara's lovers male and female, her daughters, her job, her politics, her fears, her visions. Simple, intimate and honest poetry which we identify with immediately, as it clarifies our own experience. *Illustrated; 64 pp; $1.75.*

LESSONS FROM THE DAMNED: Class Struggle in the Black Community—By The Damned. This book describes the awareness of oppression as black people, as workers and poor people under capitalism, and as women and young people oppressed by men and the family. It may be the first time that poor and petit-bourgeois black people have told their own story. *Illustrated; 160 pp; $3.25. Cloth, $7.95.*

SOME PICTURES FROM MY LIFE: A Diary—Marcia Salo Rizzi. Marcia has selected entries from her diary and combined them with her emotionally powerful ink-brush drawings—one woman's experience reflecting pictures from the lives of all women. *Illustrated; 64 pp; $1.35.*

UNBECOMING MEN: A Men's Consciousness-Raising Group Writes on Oppression and Themselves. This book reflects the struggles of a group of men who've come together because of their increasingly unavoidable awareness of sexism—how it operates against the people they most care for and ultimately, how it eats away at their own humanity. *Illustrated; 64 pp; $2.50.*

BEGIN AT START: Some Thoughts on Personal Liberation and World Change—Su Negrin. A Times Change Press editor writes about her experiences in various liberation movements (mysticism, free school, commune, new left, feminist and gay) and talks about how they're all coming together in a new way—transforming individuals and approaching a utopia more awesome than we have ever dreamed of. *Illustrated; 176 pp; $3.25. Cloth, $6.95.*

FREE OURSELVES: Forgotten Goals of the Revolution—Arthur Aron; Illustrations by Elaine N. Blesi. In our movement for social change, we have in many ways, lost touch with our humanistic values. Art believes that to realize our values we must *live* them—now—by changing ourselves and creating a giant personal/social/cultural alternative. *Illustrated; 64 pp; $1.35.*

GENERATIONS OF DENIAL: 75 Short Biographies of Women in History—Kathryn Taylor. These women were whole people under the worst of circumstances, worse still for those who, in addition to being female, were gay. These biographies are a pioneering collection with which to supplement history books and women's pride. *Illustrated; 64 pp; $2.00.*

YOUTH LIBERATION: News, Politics and Survival Information—Youth Liberation of Ann Arbor. The authors write about the oppression of being young in an adult chauvinist society—imprisonment in families and schools, economic dependence, denial of legal rights—and they describe the growing activity toward world-wide youth liberation. *Illustrated; 64 pp; $1.75.*

THE TRAFFIC IN WOMEN and Other Essays on Feminism—Emma Goldman; with a biography by Alix Kates Shulman. Emma Goldman was a dynamic anarchist and so her feminism differed markedly from her suffrage-oriented contemporaries. Today the split between liberal and radical approaches to women's liberation are still not resolved. So these essays have an uncanny relevancy to problems now being dealt with. *Illustrated; 64 pp; $2.25.*

WITH LOVE, SIRI AND EBBA—Siri Fraser and Ebba Pedersen. Siri and Ebba are two young women who decided to hitch-hike through northern Africa to Sudan and Ethiopia. These letters, drawings and photographs tell the story of their adventure and of their love for "the most fantastic free wild nomadic tribes" people, with whom they lived. *Illustrated; 128 pp; $3.25. Cloth, $8.50.*

TO ORDER ANY OF THE ABOVE BOOKS

send your order and payment

(Including 50 cents postage & handling per order;

minimum order $4.00)

to:

TIMES CHANGE PRESS

Order Department

Albion, CA 95410

Times Change Press also produces
POSTERS
They are illustrated in our free, complete catalog.

It also lists all current titles and contains fuller descriptions.

To receive a complete catalog, write to:

TIMES CHANGE PRESS

ALBION, CALIFORNIA 95410